Stick Figures

Save the World

Endorsements

How can you share Jesus with a napkin sketch and save a life? Our hearts all long for God-size stories that captivate our imagination. This handy *Stick Figures Save the World* equips us to communicate gospel stories any time, any place, and with anyone. In Sunday schools, in suburban homes, and among unreached peoples around the world, a growing movement of Jesus lovers are drawing simple stick figures to impart hope and invite people to follow him. Anyone can share Jesus with stick figures . . . so that everyone can love and obey him!

DR. MARY HO
International Executive Leader, All Nations

Dr. Pam Arlund has taken the big, scary complexity of evangelism and storytelling and simplified it in practical and important ways, so every believer can be empowered to share the good news of Jesus. *Stick Figures Save the World* is practical, inspiring, and a refreshing look at the art of storytelling. We all have good news stories to share, and this book will help you share them effectively. I highly recommend you read this, practice it, and make it part of your lifestyle.

JOSHUA JOHNSON
Co-Executive Director, All Nations Kansas City Hub

I was privileged to be mentored in this approach by Dr. Pam Arlund before our season of ministry with Middle Eastern refugees, and I am so thankful! We used the process described here to disciple many Muslim background believers and help them write the Scripture on their hearts. Pam's down-to-earth way of learning, sharing, and teaching Jesus stories is so practical and effective—and not only with those who are less literate! Every believer can use this approach to know the Word more deeply, and to be empowered to share it more widely!

MEREDITH JOHNSON
Co-Executive Director, All Nations Kansas City Hub

The pictures and the text of *Stick Figures Save the World* all proclaim, "You can do this. Don't panic because you are a bad drawer." The book is just the right length. Halfway through you might feel that there is a lot of new technique to learn, but then you see the simplicity of it and find that you can get started. I am sharpening my pencil now!

I often use illustration in teachings, because even while people copy the pictures, it helps them to remember better. In the God-is-greater-team, we also use painting as a way to remember what God is telling us. And we often find as we draw that the pictures develop even more, and the Lord continues talking.

CORA E. LUEPNITZ
Public Librarian, MA
Founder, The God-is-Greater-Team Hamburg, Germany

Recently, my church-planting team and I were trained to share the good news. At the end of this training, we began to share the good news we learned from *Stick Figures Save the World*. I shared a story that we learned during training, and it was very exciting. When I went to a beauty parlor, I suddenly met two married women that I did not know. By sharing different Bible stories using stick figures, they were very surprised to learn about the power of Jesus Christ. I think these stick figures will help you share the power of Jesus too, especially for those who are illiterate. I learned how to share everything from pictures of the Bible to the great commands of Jesus Christ!

PASTOR MOL
South Asia Ministry to Muslims

After I encountered Pam's teaching on the simple power of stick figures, I started using this method to tell stories cross-culturally to a group of Czech college girls. The students loved it, but the amazing byproduct was gaining an incredible tool to disciple my preschool-age daughter! She became fascinated by the stories and soon began to ask for them and even try to copy them. I'm so thankful that Pam's engaging book now gives more people an opportunity to share Jesus with anyone, no matter their age or cultural background!

JEAN NIES
Mom and Preschool Teacher

If you would have told me a year ago that stick figures would lead to one of the most life-giving seasons of campus ministry I've had yet, I don't know if I would have believed you. But this past year in my living room I have seen everyone from passionate atheists to church dropouts, to international students from the most unreached people groups on the planet engage with God's story in a way they may never have had if I had first opened a bible and tried to read. What's most important is that people meet the Savior for themselves, and this book will teach you a way to help people do that in way that is simple, not intimidating, reproducible, and a lot of fun!

MATT WALLIN
Campus Minister, Northern Kentucky University

Stick Figures
Save the World

Drawing Simply to Share Jesus Well

PAM ARLUND

WILLIAM CAREY PUBLISHING

Available at missionbooks.org

Published by William Carey Publishing
10 W. Dry Creek Cir
Littleton, CO 80120 | www.missionbooks.org

William Carey Publishing is a ministry of Frontier Ventures
Pasadena, CA | www.frontierventures.org

Cover and Interior Designer: Mike Riester

ISBNs: 978-1-64508-340-5 (paperback), 978-1-64508-342-9 (epub)

Printed Worldwide

26 25 24 23 22   1 2 3 4 5   IN

Library of Congress data on file with publishers.

This book is dedicated to
those who have not yet heard of Jesus
and to
those who long for everyone to know and love Jesus.

Contents

Preface

If you can check even one of the following boxes, then this book is for you:

☐ Human being

☐ Loves Jesus

☐ Loves other human beings (at least sometimes)

Did you check even one of the boxes? You did? Then keep on keeping on. This book was created for you. I promise this is going to be fun! You were made for this!

This book is for every Christian, no matter where you live and no matter where you work. Your primary workplace might be with your own kids as you educate them and help them to love and obey Jesus. Or you might be curing cancer or solving one of the mysteries of the universe. Or you might be a pastor or a missionary or a home-group leader. No matter. I hope that this book will encourage you, challenge you, inspire you, and even make you laugh. I realize that the humor in this book is probably pretty American (and likely very quirky, since it is my humor!), but I hope I can at least get you to groan and roll your eyes. I hope this book is an easy and refreshing read.

There are people in my country, the United States, who have still never really heard of Jesus. There are people in several thousand people groups around the world who have literally never heard of Jesus. If every believer would simply be a Jesus storyteller, this could change. I long to see this change. I pray to see this change.

The good news is that we don't have to be theologians to share Jesus with other people. We don't have to know apologetics to share Jesus. Having experiences with Jesus and his book, the Bible, qualify all of us to tell what we have seen and heard. Just before his ascension, Jesus promised, in Acts 1:8, that his followers would have the power to be his witnesses—not theologians or apologists, just witnesses. We simply tell what we have seen and heard and experienced of our amazing Savior, Jesus.

Now don't get me wrong, theologians and apologists (many of whom are my friends) are wonderful people, but that is not what we are all called to. We *all* are called to be Christ's witnesses. I hope this book will help train the Holy Spirit power already inside of you to be a witness to the goodness of God everywhere.

Jesus People Tell Jesus Stories. That's What Jesus People Do.

1

OK, OK. It's true—telling Jesus stories is not *all* that Jesus people do. Jesus people do all sorts of things because of our love for Jesus. In fact, you might say that living life with Jesus is really *super* awesome. Most people, when they discover something as amazing as Jesus, talk about what they have found.

If we would think for about half a second (I know it's a really long time, but hang in there!) about how humans all over the world share good news, it would probably become clear that most folks don't talk about wonderful things with long, boring, droopy faces. So talking about Jesus should definitely be more exciting than talking about the local sports team X (which shall remain unnamed, for fear of making somebody mad) or the latest movie Y (which shall also remain nameless, in case you weren't thinking of *Star* ****). Jesus is also surely more interesting than talking about the latest life-saving vitamin or a local store's 50-percent-off sale. Jesus is way more breathtaking, spine-tingling, and life-changing than anything else. The way we talk about him should show that.

Revelation 12 recounts a massive war that broke out in heaven and then continued on the earth when the "ancient serpent called the devil, or Satan, … was hurled to the earth" (v. 9). Verse 11 tells us that Jesus' faithful followers "triumphed over [the dragon] by the blood of the Lamb and by the word of their testimony." Telling

Jesus stories is equivalent to "the word of our testimony." It's simply our own personal Jesus stories. It basically means that we talk about what Jesus has done for us yesterday, the day before, last week, and last year.

Some of you might be looking forlorn and thinking, "Ah, shucks! My life is just too boring. There are no good Jesus adventures here." If we think that our own life seems a bit boring or weak on eyewitness accounts to the goodness of Jesus, there is relief for us: We can steal (i.e., borrow for a while) someone else's true tales with Jesus and tell those to other people! Then the next person will also have a new Jesus scoop to share with others. So you will have given that person several gifts: a boost to their faith, revelation of the nature of God, and the gift of interesting news to pass on (so they can be the life of the party later!).

When it comes to telling Jesus stories, we can tell how Jesus has shown up in the lives of our friends, neighbors, parents, or kids' lives. Imagine a courtroom and being a witness who gives testimony; it's simply telling other people something that we saw. So if people see God doing something really amazing for someone else, then that's one of the ways that people can give testimony. So if someone saw God heal, give care and comfort, or provide financially for someone else, then that is evidence of God moving in the world that can be passed on. Such true tales are one of the main ways people learn about God's work on earth. God's actions are not likely to be on the local newscast or in the newspaper, but God's moves are actually more significant news than what you'll normally see on TV or read in the newspaper. God invites us to be his reporters and eyewitnesses.

Sometimes we also tell Jesus stories from the Bible, which are the true tales of people we have never met. Those stories are special. Interestingly, much of the world will not believe Bible news reports, even though there is lots (and lots and lots) of proof of their historical legitimacy. However, those same people who won't believe the biblical record will have a hard time denying your own personal Jesus dispatches. It's hard for someone to accuse you of being a liar if you are passing on an event you experienced yourself! So it's important to learn to tell biblical stories (a skill we will work on together in this book), but it's also crucial to have your own personal Jesus news items ready to be told.

Quick review. Jesus stories are:
1. Real-life stuff we experienced ourselves
2. Real reports from people we know personally
3. Real reports that others shared with us
4. Events from the Bible
5. Any story anywhere on earth, since God is always present!

AUTHENTICITY

Christians are people who talk about Jesus, and not just at church. We might even talk about him *a lot*. Why? Because we want to be real about our love for him, which allows us to be real in our relationships with people. This does *not* mean trying to manipulate conversations so that we can mention Jesus every five seconds. All good things can be overdone!

Imagine that you are married or have kids or have a pet skunk or have some other super important part of your life. One day, you decide to make a new friend. Out of fear of rejection, you decide to hide that significant part of your life from your new buddy. Eight or nine months into the friendship you finally decide to reveal that very significant information to your friend. You end up saying something like, "I know this is a bit awkward, but ... Surprise! I have a spouse and a set of twins and a pet skunk too!" How would the other person react? Probably something like this: 😠.

How people react when we don't share the real us in relationships.

Of course the other person would be angry. They would think that the two of you were never real friends at all. They would be shocked so much that it might jeopardize the entire relationship. They might never trust you again. Why? Because holding back that part of yourself from the relationship violated the Principle of Authenticity.

BIG SCARY WORD

Authenticity

I'm too scared to look!

Authenticity is simply a big word that means "keeping it real." When we hide from other people the most important things in our lives, it means that we didn't engage in an honest relationship. Friendships in which we keep back the things most important to us aren't bona fide friendships, and everyone knows it. These relationships can feel slimy and yucky because they are manipulative and fake. If Jesus really is the main thing in our lives and we don't mention him, then that is a fraudulent relationship. Even people who don't follow Jesus know that.

Here's a shocker: Sometimes it's hard to be a good friend. We don't know on the front end if people will be good friends and love us back or reject us or do who-knows-what crazy thing. Jesus even talked about this problem (John 15:12–15). He says that we are supposed to love others in the same way that he loved us (v. 12). Then he spells out what he means by this: Lay down your life (v. 13) and confide in your friends (v. 15). Talking about Jesus means risking that people might not be nice and might even treat us meanly. So we put our lives on the line when we tell Jesus stories. It probably doesn't mean that we will literally get killed (but it might). Still, we risk being rejected or being embarrassed.

Most people don't like looking or feeling foolish, so they avoid having conversations about hard topics. Instead, we stick to talking about the latest Oreos flavor or the latest superhero movie. Then we wonder why we live in a generation and a country where people are depressed, isolated, and lonely.

Having courageous conversations may be difficult, but they also lead to intimacy, deep relationships, and respect based on a person's being rather than their opinions. If conversations that never go deeper than talking about cookies are good enough, then we never need risk mentioning Jesus. (It does seem appropriate to point out here that conversations about cookies, such as peanut butter, chocolate chip, snickerdoodle, oatmeal, no-bake, raisin, butter, maple, frosted, sugar, etc., can be welcome and fun. But truthfully, they should not be *all* we ever talk about. Although cookies do make people happy … Well, you get the idea.) However, if we hope for something deeper, then we will have to take a chance and broach harder topics that are closer to people's hearts.

Most of us have learned to live in a society and world in which we accept people who radically disagree with some of our viewpoints and our worldview. Many of us live in places where secular people have learned to "love their neighbor" no matter how their neighbor lives or what they believe. They have confused love with "live and let live—any way of living is healthy as long as you like it." This definition of love has confused many Christians and let the secular world define love for us. We know we need to love our neighbor, but secular people with no standards seem better at it than we are. And they seem to accept everyone—except the Christian who speaks up to share true life stories of Jesus. It's a confusing time period to live in for many.

JESUS SENDS HIS PEOPLE OUT

Happily, Jesus knew all about this time period and gave good advice on what loving relationships should look like. Before we go back to his outlook on friendship, let's look at his instructions to people going out to share about him. In Luke 10 (and Matthew 10), Jesus sends out people in pairs. Firstly, it's worth noting that we shouldn't do this alone. For all sorts of good reasons, we need to be in community. Out on the road, like they were, it might be dangerous. But most likely, when things got discouraging they would need some encouragement from a friend.

Contrary to being encouraging, Jesus sends them out like "sheep among wolves." So the modern time period is not the first time period to have a tough audience! It doesn't sound good at all, this whole "very vulnerable animal with no self-defense mechanism in the middle of scary, mean, hungry, ravenous hunters with big teeth" scenario. It's not a really great pre-short-term missions trip homily of encouragement, but naturally Jesus is being truthful.

So off the outreach team goes, and Jesus tells them what to do. He tells them to give peace to any house or village that is there. So I imagine a hippy with a peace symbol on his shirt, saying, "Hey, dude—Peace!" But all too often believers don't bring peace into relationships. Instead, sometimes, we bring hostility, hurt, confusion, and defensiveness into relationships. With those things as a starter, a good relationship is nigh impossible. Even if people are in obviously harmful lifestyles (to themselves or others), we should always come in peace.

If we come in peace, that changes the nature of everything. Even if the wolves are all around us, we are simply sheep. Sheep are simple, nonthreatening, soft, cute animals. This is the model Jesus gave us in relationships with other human beings.

SHEEP** AMONG WOLVES

*Hey, they are cute and easy to draw!

In Luke 10, if the believers are accepted in peace and are welcomed, then they should stay and hang out with those people. After eating (it's really nice that Jesus included this step, as eating is usually fun, especially if there are cookies or maybe ice cream or maybe ice cream with cookies in it), then we are to become agents of healing. We let people know that the source of the healing is from God. This healing can be a miraculous physical or emotional healing through the laying on of hands. It might also be sharing about how to let one's heart or life be healed through God. Being agents of healing can sometimes be slow work, but Jesus tells us to test for openness to peace and healing. If there is no receptivity to Jesus or our peace-and-healing way of life, Jesus tells the believers on the team to shake the dust and move on.

Wait a minute. … Are we really just supposed to "move on" when people are not interested in the way of living Jesus offers? It certainly appears that way. Now there are all sorts of misconceptions about what departing might look like. In the original text of Luke 10, Jesus instructs the short-term missions team to tell the people the consequences of their rejection of Jesus. The words there are pretty strong, beginning with something like "Woe unto you!" Proclaiming a pox or a curse upon someone was a bit more like normal conversation in Jesus' day than ours (albeit still not that normal). In our day and age, declaring calamity is something pretty much reserved for bad movies about King Arthur or Robin Hood or maybe something from Shakespeare (but clearly one of his dramas in which everyone dies, and not a comedy). "Woe unto you …" might sound sophisticated in a school play, but it probably won't go over so well in a coffee shop in the modern world.

So what would be the functional equivalent of declaring the consequences of a bad life choice but leaving someone to make their own choices? (In other words, what would be the modern equivalent and application of Luke 10:10–15?) Perhaps it would sound something like, "I can see that you are not interested in Jesus right now. It's a shame. I can tell you from experience that life will improve and will be better if you follow him. I don't want to force you into anything you aren't ready for, but I know that a life without him is difficult. So I'll leave it be for now and maybe we'll circle back around to Jesus at another time, when you are ready." Then we go home and pray for that person, live an authentic life before them, and let the Holy Spirit do his work.

By the way, knowing the difference between God's work and our work is key here. Many times the Bible talks about "ripe fruit" when it talks about people who are open to Jesus (see John 15:16; Matthew 13:1–9). Jesus made it clear that not everyone would be open to him. It's sad, but it's true.

Now where I come from, it is absolutely essential to grow tomatoes in the summertime. The point of growing the tomatoes is not to eat them. No, the point of the tomatoes is to have something to talk about. So everything I know about agriculture (horticulture, agronomy, or farming, etc.) comes from the few tomato plants we had in our backyard in the suburbs.

Now I hate eating tomatoes, but growing them was exciting. The only problem is that five-year-old me would go out there *every* day and look at them. The stupid things were so slow in growing. It was frustrating. I wanted to speed them along, you know?

So my little-girl mind became fixated on watching one particular tomato and measuring it (very scientifically, of course) daily. I looked at it, I petted it, I measured it. I waited and tenderly cared for it. Then one day while it was still green, the tomato next to it (the one I had not been paying attention to) suddenly went plop and fell to the ground.

The tomato on the ground was now a shriveled-up mess of yuckiness. It had been ripe, but I missed it! I was so focused on the one little tomato, trying to get it to grow, that I missed the tomato right next to it.

The deep message that nearly slipped by city-slicker me would have been obvious to an agricultural audience. Hyper-focusing on one tomato (a person who is not open to Jesus) means we might miss other tomatoes that are ready to be harvested (people that are open and ready to meet Jesus). In other words, the best way to insure a big, full harvest is to check on ripeness and then move on when people are not ready yet. We come back and check on them later. We may even fertilize it a bit by sharing a bit more, but we don't stop looking at all the other tomatoes that are also trying to grow.

For my fellow city slickers, let me make this little story clear. Jesus says that it's his job (not ours) to prepare hearts to be open to him (Mark 4:26–29). So we can simply move on when people are not open and keep looking for those who are. We can check back and share a bit more with people, pray for them, offer his healing. However, it's his job to help people to be open. We can't do that. Isn't that freeing?

Oh, here's the other bit of good news in this too: Not everyone we share Jesus with will be ready to talk about him, and it doesn't necessarily mean we did anything wrong! Now sure, we might have done something wrong; but not necessarily so.

Jesus says our job is to spread seed (Mark 4:3, 26). He says we don't even have to worry about where we spread it. Jesus said that the farmer in his story even spread seed on the footpath. Now, when I have asked farmers about this, they say, "That's stupid! Seed costs money. You don't throw seed everywhere. That's bad farming." Now city-slicker you and me might not have realized that, but Jesus' original hearers would have known that almost for sure.

Why would Jesus have us throw seed on the footpath, where it seems obvious it won't grow? Because sometimes it grows! Ask my mother as she is out trying to kill seeds that grow up in our sidewalk and in our driveway. My mother has an ongoing fight with those stupid plants that grow up in the crack in our driveway. She roots them out and she sprays them, but then they grow back anyway.

I think Jesus told us to throw our seed everywhere because we are clueless. People who are open to hearing about Jesus could be anywhere and look like anything. We have a tendency to try to judge whether people will be open to Jesus by how they look. So we make decisions for them. We decide, "Oh, they surely aren't open to Jesus. I won't even bother to try to share with them." Then boom—we just took away their choice.

So Jesus said not to try to be a super-strategic sharer of this really amazing news. He said to just share it everywhere with everyone. Then once we've done that, he does the rest. He is the one who makes it grow—or not (Mark 4:27–28).

Jesus made the terms of friendship clear. He said that when he shared with us all that God has shown him, we became his friends (John 15:15). In fact, Jesus said that when he withheld information from us, we had a master-slave relationship with him. He said that the difference between the master-slave relationship and the friend-friend relationship was a confiding, a sharing of knowledge, a sharing of life.

HOW TO BE A GOOD FRIEND

Likewise, when we share everything that God has shown us with others, this establishes friendships. Maybe it's because if we don't pass on potentially useful information, we have denied people the right to decide for themselves what to do with that information. We've denied them a basic human right of choice. Which means we've put ourselves in the position of power over someone else—i.e., a master. No wonder holding back on information doesn't meet Jesus' definition of friendship. Keeping it real means risking sharing this amazing Jesus with others and then letting them decide whether or not they would also like to follow him. Authentic love is hard sometimes. (Well, almost all the time, if I'm keeping it real!)

Let's make this clear by using a simple example. Let's say I am making a bad fashion choice. For me, a really bad fashion choice would be skinny jeans. (Curvy jeans might be better for me. Just sayin'.) My female friends see me looking awkward in my skinny jeans, but they decide to say nothing. They interpret friendship as saying nothing, and so they remain silent about my skinny jeans and talk about cookies instead. Then all night long people snicker and point at me behind my back due to the complete ridiculousness of me in skinny jeans. Were they being good friends? No! Let me be very clear on this: NO!!!! They were *not* being good friends.

On the other hand, let's say I show up in my skinny jeans (which I'm sure are perfectly fine for you, but let me reemphasize here that curvy is more my shape). And my friends notice my poor choice. They also would not say, "Those jeans are dumb. They are evil. They are wrong. You can't wear those. You must stop right now or else I will never be your friend. In fact, if you don't take off those skinny jeans, we can never be real friends. And every time we meet, I will bring up your evil skinny jeans again and again until you finally realize the error of your ways."

I will (I can guarantee it) cry, and then never talk to that "friend" again. For sure.

On the other hand, a true friend could say, "You know, skinny jeans are not healthy or good, especially not for you. There are some other really cool fashions that might bring out the real you, you know, the curvy and amazing you whom God created. This way of living is not right for you (or anyone else in your circumstances, most likely). Want to go shopping?"

In this case, I might say, "Forget it. I like my skinny jeans." In which case, my friend would be forced to live with me and the skinny jeans and the ghastly sight before their eyes until I saw the true light of repentance. Even if I said to leave me alone about my jeans, though, we'd still be friends. And later, upon closer thought, I might wake up and realize that my friends were right and ask them where to shop.

On the other hand, I might immediately say something like, "Really? I was thinking skinny jeans were cool. But they *are* tight and uncomfortable, now that you mention it. Are there other cool jeans out there? Where do I get them? You promise I'll look good in them? Show me the way."

And voila—we are now much closer friends, and the world is improved dramatically by getting me out of skinny jeans and into something more appropriate for me. (I know that people who don't care for cookies can wear skinny jeans, but you already know how I feel about cookies.)

If I know there is something out there that would really help you, but I withhold it and don't even offer it to you, I'm not a friend. I'm a master. I have taken control of your life and withdrawn the right of choice from you. In politics, that's called a colonial relationship. If I come along and take choices away from you, then I'm a colonizer, a lord, a boss. So anyone who says that people who have never heard about Jesus should just be "left alone" has decided for that people group that they should not hear about Jesus and thus is a colonizer and a master—not a friend.

We intuitively know this definition of master to be true. Imagine the situation in which your friend watches you struggle with life. They listen to you and watch you, but that's it. Then one day you discover that they knew the exact solution to your problem and never recommended it to you. You would likely question whether that person was your friend at all.

Likewise, what if your friend recommended a solution that you didn't like? If they kept pursuing it anyway, trying to force the solution on you, then you would also question the relationship. You might even say, "Quit trying to be the boss of me!" You would recognize that the relationship wasn't friendship but a boss (master)-client relationship instead.

Good friends inform their buddies about potential solutions and then leave the choices to them. That's an authentic relationship, just the kind that Jesus wants.

So at this point there are probably three types of reactions to this book (I won't mention the people who already quit reading!):

1. The Shouldn'ts: People who follow Jesus, but who think that sharing Jesus is wrong and shouldn't be done.

2. The Couldn'ts: People who follow Jesus, but don't know how to share him with others or aren't sure it's their job.

3. The Woo-hoos: People who are super pumped and ready to get on with finding out how stick figures can save the world.

I have written a brief letter to members of each group.

LETTER # I—TO THE SHOULDN'TS

Dear person who follows Jesus, but thinks that sharing Jesus is wrong and shouldn't be done:

I hear you. Maybe you've had some bad experiences and you assume that others have too. You think, "They don't want to talk about Jesus." And that might be true, but then again it might not. Why should we assume that people don't want to talk about Jesus? Many people like to have real conversations about real things. So rather than assuming that people don't want to talk about Jesus, maybe it would be better not to make assumptions. And maybe having Jesus conversations will help avoid having one more superficial, boring, plasticky, not-adding-up-to-anything kind of conversation in life. Please rescue us all from those kinds of conversations!

One (possibly brilliant) idea would be to do less talking altogether and ask more questions about the other person. (This is especially brilliant if you are an introvert or shy by nature—which, by the way, is *not* a "get-out-of-evangelism-free" card. Get this: When you are authentic, you get to have Jesus conversations *and* let the other person do most of the talking. Now that's a win-win!) For example, ask people if they've ever heard of Jesus. Ask them what they know about Jesus and what they think about Jesus. Then ask them why they think what they think. Maybe you could just try to be a person that asks good questions. Then, see where the conversation goes from there.

That's an authentic relationship. In the modern world, people are rarely asked their opinions and then really listened to. Maybe people would like it if others asked their opinion on real-life issues and then listened.

Let's be clear: I'm not even talking about (gasp!) *evangelism* as you are probably thinking of it.

So let's talk about the elephant in the room. (Snarky side note: That nifty expression means "Let's talk about the thing we all know about, but no one is mentioning out loud." It's an odd phrase, since where I come from there has never been an actual elephant in any room, and I can't imagine that it has *ever* happened that people have been in a room with an elephant and not mentioned it. … But I digress.)

Why did evangelism get a bad rap anyway? Maybe it became like a competition. Like something you could win. Maybe it was something that people just did like a machine, as if you typed a code into a computer and followers of Jesus would just pop out of the printer. That kind of stinkin' thinkin' meant that evangelism turned flat-out yucky sometimes. Thinking like that meant that people somehow forgot that not all people are the same. We forgot authenticity. So no wonder no one really liked that.

Some people like one thing and others like another. Some people even like to mix fruit in with their tea (gasp!), and we have to learn to love them too! So I'm not talking about a one-size-fits-all, let's-get-people-through-our-method-and-check-the-box-and-be-done kind of thing. Nope. That's not it at all.

Evangelism is simply sharing Jesus and ourselves with people. It can sometimes mean reaching out to new people we've never met. And that's scary. (Not-so-snarky side note: Let's face it, people and relationships are scary. We never really know what will happen in them.) But evangelism simply gives people a basic right to say yes or no to Jesus. Neither evangelism nor real Jesus friendships require anyone to follow Jesus. But if people never even get the chance to say yes to Jesus, then that's not fair or right. Everyone should get the chance to make their own choice. So evangelism offers people the chance to make a choice, but only if we keep it real ourselves and share who he is and what he means to us.

Maybe we need to talk a bit about unconditional love here. It seems like this concept should be straightforward, but it sure does seem like it got all mixed up. Unconditional love means "I love you no matter what you do." There is some truth in that statement. However, it's not a full biblical understanding of love. But then what does love mean? Without going into the different Greek words for love (which is not necessary) or writing a five-hundred-page treatise on love (which might be cool to about two people in the world), love is simply that Golden Rule thing. Way back when I was in school, my teachers said it like this: "Treat others as you would like to be treated." By the way, the Golden Rule is straight from Jesus (Matthew 7:12; Luke 6:31). So we can still be kind to others, even if they are not kind to us.

This unconditional love thing doesn't mean that we let people make poor life choices and say and do nothing about it. It does mean that you try your best to notice, listen, and be kind to someone in a way that makes sense to that other person. It also means that we offer friendship and the best advice we have to offer. And for us, the best advice we have to offer is Jesus' way. If they reject Jesus' way, we still keep open the possibility of friendship. For example, I will still love you even if you put fruit in your tea. Fruit-tea drinkers need Jesus too! That's love without condition.

Love without advice for better living is not love at all. Love doesn't just watch a friend (or enemy, since we have to love them too!) make really terrible life decisions and stand by and say and do nothing. That's called indifference—not love.

Love means offering God and God solutions to people and then not slamming the door on potential relationships, even if they reject God. Jesus said that he told his disciples everything the Father told him, and he called the result friendship. What if we defined friendship in the same way? It would mean that the stuff we receive from Jesus, we pass on. That sounds nice.

Good friends (and sometimes total strangers) offer advice about life, everything from what to wear to what to eat to who to date. So why wouldn't Jesus people share their thoughts on things little and big even when people reject Jesus' advice about sexual relationships, marriage, handling money, and all sorts of really important things?

But true friends still offer advice and then let their friends decide whether or not to take the advice. That's respect.

By the way, we are still in relationship with people whom we live in society with but do not personally know. The idea that we can be indifferent to our neighbors just because we don't know them was one of the ideas that Jesus blew out of the water. Jesus said to care for strangers (and he didn't mean your odd friend who wears flamingo slippers or drinks fruit tea). He meant that we have to care for people we don't even know. So sometimes he will ask us to try to initiate loving conversations with strangers. In fact, he seems to say that being kind to strangers was especially hard and therefore especially awesome.

Somehow people think that talking about Jesus is not allowed in the postmodern world. You know, that's the world that tries to make it seem like we're all atheists while we're out in public. (Talk about lacking authenticity!) And some workplaces and schools have even tried to make rules about these things. Depending on where you live, such rules might even be illegal in and of themselves. Anyway, you might not be able to share in that environment right away. But if you pray and ask and stay aware, eventually an opportunity will be given to you. Even in the most oppressive environments on earth this is true. And when the opportunity to share Jesus comes up (and it will likely be obvious that it has), then break the rules and share Jesus anyway. (There, I just gave you permission to be a rule-breaker!) You might lose your job or get kicked out of school, but that's unlikely if you are actually sharing in love.

On the other hand, if the other person says that there is no way for you to get to talk about Jesus ever, then you might not be in an authentic relationship after all. It's good to know that and maybe even to have some real conversation about that. Maybe if that person is your grandma, you just have to deal with it and love her as best you can. But if it's a person you are hanging out with and they won't let you share your real life, then that person is probably not ready for authenticity in relationship. If so, you can (and most definitely should) pray for them, but you will have to wait for the Holy Spirit to make them ready.

Sincerely yours,
Stick-Figure Drawer

LETTER #2—TO THE COULDN'TS

Dear person who follows Jesus, but just doesn't think you know how to share him with others:

Thanks for your honesty. I really appreciate it. The good news is that this book is here to help. And there is other good news too! Jesus never asked us to spread theology. He simply asked us to be witnesses. So you can just tell what you know and what you've heard. We can pass on the stories of how Jesus changed us, our kids, our grandkids, our neighbors, and even the previously cranky man across the street.

Sharing the Bible doesn't have to be that hard. We think that we have to use big and complicated words to sound important. But that's not true. The truth of Jesus is simple and totally awesome. We just have to pass on the stories that we know. We just share stories from the Bible that have changed us. That's not so hard. In fact, if you know some big words related to the Bible, it really would be better if you didn't use them. It's not that they are totally useless. It's just that they are not the best words for sharing Jesus with practically anybody. Since you don't know what they mean and the other person doesn't know what they mean, let's just not use them! Don't you feel lighter already?

Here's a little secret: The best words with the strongest meaning are short words—not long words. So if you want to tell stories in super-cool ways, use the shortest words you can—not the longest ones. It's so true and so freeing. Shorter words actually make better stories. (I know this advice is super disappointing to the three of you who know how to properly use the word *soteriology*. Knowing words like that is not bad, not at all. But using words like that to share Jesus with people is actually *not* good. The rest of us are just "getting saved," and that works just fine.)

Q: Which word should I use in my story: brobdingnagian OR big?

A: Short, simple words are better and happier!

I'm going to make a radical guess here that I'm sure is true for your "friend," but certainly not for you: Your "friend" might be a bit shy or socially awkward. So how can you help your "friend"? There's so much good news here. Firstly, true confessions: I'm shy and socially awkward, but I've shared Jesus with lots of people. Secondly, if you are already feeling a bit out of step socially, then it might make sharing Jesus easier. If people can see that it's hard for you, then they will see that you are doing it out of lovingkindness. And you can learn to be a really good question-asker and listener. Later on, this book will help you learn how to start conversations. That might seem awkward at first, as any new skill is hard and weird. But if you're already used to such things being hard, then it's just another day in your normal life, right? Oh, oops, I mean in your "friend's" life …

By the time you get to the end of this book, you will better know how to share Jesus with others. You won't have to do it in some canned and mechanical way. You get to be you! So that means you won't mess it up. And if you do find a way to mess it up, then you get forgiven and taught by Jesus to do it better next time. There's so much grace from Jesus.

This book is here to help. So you are in exactly the right place. Keep reading!

Sincerely yours,
Stick-Figure Drawer

LETTER #3—TO THE WOO-HOOS

Dear person who is super pumped and ready to get on with finding out how stick figures can save the world:

Thanks for your patience. We are about to get there. Glad you are excited! I promise it won't take long to get going on to the nitty gritty of how to do it.

And maybe less caffeine would be good for you? Just a friendly suggestion.

Sincerely yours,
Stick-Figure Drawer

2 Jesus Told Stories, You Should Too.

> Jesus used many similar stories and illustrations to teach the people as much as they could understand. In fact, in his public ministry he never taught without using parables; but afterward, when he was alone with his disciples, he explained everything to them.
>
> (Mark 4:33–34)

So I'm going to be *very* truthful with you here. Every single point I am about to make in this next little section is already right there, in that passage of Scripture. Pretty much says it all: Jesus used stories so people could understand, and he did it a lot. Done. End of story.

So if you want to, you can just skip on down to the next section. (When was the last time a book's author was *that* honest with you, hmm? I wish some of my college textbooks had said, "This whole book is basically useless, why don't you just skip me?" That would have been nice.)

However (what a mighty word!), … if you are a curious, restless soul who amazingly and relentlessly seeks out the story behind the story (the context), then there just *might* be some good stuff here in this section. Or if you are a skeptic, thinking this whole book is just nonsense, this next section just *might* help you see that I've done my homework (even when it wasn't fun).

And maybe this section will even be interesting. … You'll never know unless you read on. Maybe you should just try a little? Just a bit might be interesting, you know. Or maybe *all* of it will be interesting? Perhaps …

Imagine the scene in Mark 4 (and Matthew 13). Jesus the miracle healer and confronter of legalism is gaining in popularity. In fact, he is so popular that crowds are often coming to check him out. We know that this particular day was not the first time he had taught by the lakeshore, because Mark's Gospel says, "Once again Jesus began teaching by the lakeshore" (Mark 4:1). That nifty phrase, "once again," means it had happened before. So not rocket science so far.

On this particular occasion, so many people are gathered around hoping to hear or see Jesus that he pushes a (likely small) boat just offshore and sits down in it. Jesus has the chance to say anything he wants to the waiting crowds. So what does Jesus do? "He taught them by telling many stories in the form of parables" (Mark 4:2).

He tells them a story about a farmer scattering seed in a field. And then, when he's done, he says, "Anyone with ears to hear should listen and understand" (Mark 4:9). He doesn't explain the story. He just ends. Cut! End of story. Done.

If I were there, I'm sure I would have been confused. I would have thought, "Well, isn't that a sweet story? But I don't have any idea what it's all about. Maybe I should go get some cookies while I think about it." It's confusing. It leaves me wondering what the crowd thought about the story, but we'll never know. Perhaps they understood the scenario better than I do, because although Jesus' behavior is likely unusual to modern people (like me), his behavior wasn't at all odd in the first-century Jewish environment in which he lived.

WHEN JESUS WENT TO "SCHOOL"

Keep in mind that Jesus grew up in a Jewish community in a Jewish household. Most of us today have no idea what school looked like in those days. We imagine it to be like we experienced in the modern world, but it was really quite different. By the time kids like Jesus finished "elementary school," they likely had all or part of the first five books of the Bible memorized. I hate to think about what the kids at our local elementary school have memorized, but I can pretty much guarantee that none of them have memorized Genesis, Exodus, Leviticus, Numbers, and Deuteronomy.

Normally, a Jewish boy would go to his first Passover in Jerusalem at around the age of twelve or thirteen. When Jesus went to his first Passover in Jerusalem (at age twelve), his level of education up to that point was made evident by Luke 2:46–47: "Three days later they [Joseph and Mary] finally discovered him [Jesus] in the Temple, sitting among the religious teachers, listening to them and asking questions. All who heard him were amazed at his understanding and his answers."

The rabbis (whom we would call teachers) would "hint" (*remez* in Hebrew, if you want to sound cool) at part of a Scripture passage, and then the student was supposed to know the rest of the passage. That is how the educational system worked in first-century Judaism. Often the teacher would quote a verse before or after the relevant passage and the student was expected to know the rest.

This reminds me of a game I once played with some Mennonites during a blizzard in Kansas. We were snowbound with nothing to do. So we played Bible trivia, in which the players of the game tried to ask questions that would stump the other players of the game, without accessing a printed Bible at all. What was embarrassing about this game was that I was the visiting "Bible teacher" and I got totally whipped by the thirteen-year-old in the game. (He knew way too much about bears and the dangers of insulting prophets, for example. Never underestimate the power of a young mind. But I digress ...)

A first-century student was also expected to ask good questions, to seek out the rest of the answer that the teacher had hinted at. This was especially true if the teacher had told a story that he had just made up. And first-century teachers made up a lot of stories. There are more than 3,500 parables from first-century rabbis that still exist![1] In general, about one-third of Jesus' teachings are parables—i.e., stories that Jesus made up to illustrate a point. In fact, some of our favorite stories never really happened. The story of the Prodigal Son (Luke 15:11–32) and the Good Samaritan (Luke 10:25–37) are not historical accounts. They are parables, or stories, that Jesus made up to make a point.

It was common, and even normal, in the education system for Jesus to wait to see who would remain behind to ask questions to reveal the fullness of the "hints" he was dropping. In this way, the teacher could see who was hungry for more knowledge and who was dedicated. In this case, the twelve disciples

---

1 Ray Vander Laan, "Rabbi and Talmidim," That the World May Know Ministries, https://www.thattheworldmayknow.com/rabbi-and-talmidim.

knew this system, so they hung around for a full revelation of the story that Jesus was telling, and they received their explanation in due time.

Next Jesus tells a parable about a lamp on a stand. Then he repeats the phrase, "Anyone with ears to hear should listen and understand" (Mark 4:23). Then he explains the *kingdom economy of learning* (Mark 4:24–25). Essentially, if you listen to a bit of Jesus' teaching and then listen closer, you will be given more teaching and more understanding. But if someone is not really listening, then what little they have will also be removed.

This kingdom economy of learning is still at work today. When you share Jesus stories with people, pay attention to see if they *lean in* and show interest or if they *lean out*, indicating they *aren't ripe yet*. Jesus tells us that the harvest is ripe, so we need to make sure that we are *checking the fruit* to see which ones are ripe for his message.

Jesus is also an example to us in how to pace the information shared with the listener. Mark explains to us that Jesus used many stories and parables to teach the people as much as they could understand. In fact, his normal method was to teach in public and then later explain the stories more fully to his disciples. Notice that the crowds did not receive the explanations to the stories. People would have to stay behind and ask questions later to hear the explanations.

So it seems that Jesus was doing several things here by his storytelling:

1. Teaching the crowds as much as they could understand (Mark 4:33)
2. Giving explanations to smaller groups that would stay with him and ask questions (Mark 4:10–20, 34; Matt 13:10, 36–43)
3. Building upon people's ability to listen to ramp up to more and more understanding for those who had the capacity to understand more (Mark 4:25; Matt 13:12)

Notice how Eugene Peterson, translator of *The Message* version of the Bible, translates Matthew 13:13:

> That's why I tell stories: to create readiness, to nudge the people toward receptive insight. In their present state they can stare till doomsday and not see it, listen till they're blue in the face and not get it.

To expand on the idea a bit, look at how Peterson translates Mark 4:33:

> With many stories like these, he [Jesus] presented his message to them, fitting the stories to their experience and maturity.

In other words, using stories that reflected their experience and their maturity (their understanding level so far) was the best way for people to learn as much as they were ready and able to learn at that point. For those who were already followers, Jesus sometimes preached sermons or gave explanations of Scripture or theology; but for those who were still coming toward him and maybe couldn't understand much yet, Jesus' best tool was storytelling.

If Jesus felt that storytelling was such a great tool for adults and children alike, then why do we use it so rarely in the modern world? The parables that he told were for adults. The idea that storytelling was for the children's Sunday school class but not for the adults' class was nowhere in Jesus' paradigm. In fact, there is no recorded incident of Jesus ever teaching a crowd that was comprised *only* of children. When children are mentioned, they have been learning alongside adults.

WHAT WE CAN LEARN FROM MODERN NEUROSCIENCE

There is nothing childish about teaching through stories. In fact, the "hint" method of telling stories and then inviting the hearers to gather understanding and ask good questions is quite an advanced method of teaching—one that is being redeemed in the modern world, thanks to MRI imagery. Neuroscience is now showing us that telling stories changes how people think, feel, and behave.[2] It turns out that stories are better than lectures at helping people to learn. I love it when science "figures out" what Jesus already knew, and the Bible already demonstrated—don't you?

Long before there was such a thing as "educational theory," God understood how the human brain worked. He did create the human brain, so it makes sense.

Now even though we all have a brain, most of us are not aware of how it works or how it learns anything new. As a result, you might have read this far, and you are still a skeptic about this whole stick figure thing. It might seem too childish for your brain. I get it. I used to be like you.

---

2 Here are a couple of references among the thousands that could be offered here: Annie Murphy Paul, "Your Brain on Fiction," *The New York Times*, Opinion section, March 17, 2012, https://www.nytimes.com/2012/03/18/opinion/sunday/the-neuroscience-of-your-brain-on-fiction.html; M. Glaser, B. Garsoffky, and S. Schwan, "Narrative-Based Learning: Possible Benefits and Problems," *Communications* 34 (2009): 429–47.

I went to the mission field thinking I was destined to be a great missionary. I mean, I just knew I was. I'm sure every missionary thinks that, especially if they are as young as I was at the time! Jesus sent me to work with a Muslim people group who had never had any interaction with the Bible and had no writing system for their language. So my job was to help them make a choice about Jesus. The choice was and is theirs to make, but they simply didn't have the tools to make any real choice.

The question was: *What tools would I use to help them discover Jesus?* I like to read, but I knew right away that books were probably not going to be their thing. Don't get me wrong—they were intelligent people, but they weren't book people. They knew how to live in a harsh highland environment, and they knew how to get around the government to live their lives as they wanted. They taught me many skills that I didn't have, like how to build a house out of mud, how to ride a camel, how to make bread, how to read the weather patterns, and how to jump across frozen rivers. No doubt, they were intelligent.

I gave them beautiful copies of parts of the Bible in a trade language that many of them were pretty good at. They took one look at them and put them in their pockets, and I never saw them again. That was frustrating.

Then I brought in beautiful pictures and began to tell them the stories of the Bible. They got a little too interested in the pictures and didn't think much about the stories. Finally, I took out an old pen and a ratty piece of paper and drew some stick figures on it and told a story from the Bible. I told many Jesus stories from my own life too. Then I waited to see what happened. And, like we saw with Jesus in the Gospels, they began to ask questions about the story. A few hours later I saw some kids drawing the stick figures for other kids and telling them the story.

Eureka! I went home and began to draw stick figures and practice. I found out that I was learning my Bible better than ever, and so were they. I began to realize how people learn. For me, it wasn't that I couldn't read and write. It wasn't that I couldn't interact with difficult texts. It was simply that drawing stick figures was actually *better* than the traditional Bible-study methods I had been taught.

It turns out that this simple stick figure method is basically better for all human beings. Any person at any level of understanding has the opportunity to lean in and ask more questions. And I'm guessing that you are a human being if you are reading this book.

LOVING ORAL LEARNERS

If, indeed, you are a human being, then you likely prefer to learn in some way other than reading and writing. If you look at literacy scores reported by countries around the world, it looks like most people can read and write. However, if we switch to looking at how well people can actually learn from print, then roughly half of the adults in the world can't learn well from texts. This means that something like 50 percent of the residents of our planet likely struggle a lot when trying to learn from books, while another 35 percent can read but would likely prefer a different way to learn. In fact, only 10 percent scored in the top category of people who do really well with reading and writing.[3] All of the other people are called oral preference learners. It's not that people absolutely can't read and write in most cases. It's that they prefer to learn in some other way. Put together, that means 85 percent of the world will likely struggle with reading through a print version of the Bible.

So then, that's a problem, right? I hope you agree with me that the Bible is not only helpful but absolutely necessary for following Jesus (the way a universal communicator is essential to *Star Trek* personnel, perhaps?). If people either can't or won't read the Scriptures, then what do we do? Here's the really cool thing … We do exactly what the people who lived in Jesus' day did! They shared the stories of Jesus from person to person. How do we know this? Luke explains it to us! The problem is that the explanation is in a part of the Bible we usually consider boring and sort of skip over to get on to the good stuff, so to speak. Hang in there with me for a minute. It's really cool.

---

3 Organisation for Economic Cooperation and Development, "Skills Matter: Additional Results from the Survey of Adult Skills," OECD Skills Studies, 2019, https://doi.org/10.1787/1f029d8f-en.

Now remember, Luke was a doctor. Even in his day, doctors were highly educated people. He was the crème de la crème (that makes me think of ice cream!) of the reading society in his day. He wrote two books of the Bible, which comprise a two-volume work. The first volume is called Luke and the second volume is called Acts. (Why, oh why, is our Bible organized with John in between them so that we forget they are a two-volume work?!)

Luke told us how he went about writing his two books:

> Many people have set out to write accounts about the events that have been fulfilled among us. They used the *eyewitness reports circulating among us from the early disciples.* Having carefully investigated everything from the beginning, I also have decided to write an accurate account for you, most honorable Theophilus, so you can be certain of the truth of everything you were taught. (Luke 1:1–4)

Whoa! Wait a minute! They were telling Jesus stories that they had heard from people who had been there and personally witnessed the events recorded in the Gospel of Luke? Yep. That's what Luke meant when he mentioned "eyewitness reports circulating among us from the early disciples." In other words, Jesus people were telling Jesus stories, because that's what Jesus people do! For a bare minimum of thirty years from the days of Jesus to the days when Luke was writing his book, people had been telling Jesus stories from person to person.

This was no game of telephone. Do you know that game? If not, it works like this: People line up in a row, and the first person whispers a message directly into the ear of the next person. (In really mean versions of the game, the second person isn't allowed to have the message repeated. If they didn't hear it, then they just didn't hear it.) Then the second person turns and whispers what they thought they heard to the next person. This process continues down the line or around the circle.

For an example, let's say the first person whispers this message into the second person's ear: "Chocolate chip cookies are the best and should be consumed daily for good health. On the other hand, peanut butter cookies are good too, especially when consumed while watching *Star Trek*."

By the time the message comes out the other end, the message ends up something horrible like: "Chocolate chip cookies are bad for you and should not be consumed *ever*. On your feet, peanut butter is bad for you, and so is *Star Wars*."

That's so terrible!!! And it's nothing like how the stories were being told from person to person in Luke's day. People cared about these stories. They worked to preserve them accurately. When people got them wrong, the others would have corrected them. This is the way storytelling worked in first-century Judaism and how storytelling works in oral cultures today. The community values the stories, so they work hard to keep them accurate.

Oh, and one more bit of good news for us all: The Bible itself does not say that faith comes from reading the Bible! Come on, you likely know what it says: "So faith comes from hearing, that is, hearing the Good News about Christ" (Rom 10:17).

Now don't get me wrong here. I *love* reading. I thank the Lord that I can read the Bible and that I live in a time period where it is easy to get a Bible. Before the invention of the printing press, it was basically impossible for all believers to have their own Bible. I am so blessed. But there are so many other ways to get the content of the Bible into us.

Having another believer tell us orally what happened is the original way that people got this amazing book into them. In fact, telling stories from person to person actually increases healing of our hearts and builds Jesus community (church) in a way that nothing else does.[4] In other words, telling Jesus stories to each other actually has benefits that reading the Bible alone does not have.

4 Curt Thompson, *Anatomy of the Soul: Surprising Connections between Neuroscience and Spiritual Practices That Can Transform Your Life and Relationships* (Carol Stream, IL: Tyndale Momentum, 2010 [Kindle Location: 160, pp. 4, 74, 77, 78]).

I have been involved in translating the Bible into a small minority language of Central Asia. I want the Bible to be available in every language. However, many languages currently have no writing system. So what do we do? We tell Jesus stories person to person, and we make audio recordings of the Bible. For sure we all need God and his book (the Bible) inside of us. However, reading his book is not the only way to learn it.

If you are really good with books—congratulations! I love books too! Now let's learn how to be helpful and bless all the peoples of the earth by learning how to tell Jesus stories in a way that everyone can take in. You could even think of it as using "your freedom to serve one another in love" (Gal 5:13).

STORIES ARE SUPERHEROES!

Really cool scientists have done really cool experiments on the human brain. In one study, they monitored people's brains as the people watched a James Bond movie.[5] (Why wasn't I smart enough to get a job where they paid me to watch movies?!) While the people watched the movie, their hearts raced and their pulse rates went up when old 007 was in danger, even though *everyone* knows that 007 could not possibly die in the movie! Everyone knows that the main character is always indestructible. (Woe be to the nameless redshirts in *Star Trek*; they are *always* dead by the end of the show!)

Still, people got into Bond—James Bond's—well-being. Viewers were worried about Bond and his life. They were so worried, as a matter of fact, that their brains started releasing oxytocin. Interestingly, oxytocin is a neurochemical

---

5 Jeffrey Zacks, *Flicker: Your Brain on Movies* (Oxford and New York: Oxford University Press, 2014). [All of Part 1 of his book is relevant to this discussion.]

that makes a person feel safe.[6] This doesn't happen when people lecture, but it does happen when people tell stories. This means that storytellers gain more trust and are therefore remembered better than lecturers. People who trust the storyteller are also more likely to take whatever actions the storyteller might suggest.

Jesus is certainly one to be remembered. He wants us to follow him and live as he shows us. He knew that stories would help achieve that end better than lectures.

In recent years, the business world has really caught on to this emphasis on storytelling. It's caught on so much that the Harvard Business School is talking about it a lot.[7] People are even teaching business workshops on how to use stick figures to sell your product (see Dan Roam's books, for example[8]).

So stick figures and storytelling are definitely not just for the peewee Sunday school class or the children's sermon. And they aren't simply for people who can't read and write very well. Some of the richest and most powerful people in the world are catching on to what Jesus already knew. If big business can learn to cooperate with God's design of the human brain, then how much more should believers cooperate with that design?

YOU CAN BE A SUPERHERO TYPE OF PERSON TOO!

Stories are super powerful. They are so awesomely powerful that we willingly spend hours and hours with them—especially when they are told to us in movies or by other people. So it totally makes sense that stories are the best way to tell the best true story ever told: The Jesus Story. No, not just the story of Jesus while he was on earth—but the whole story, from the beginning to the end of the whole world. (Sounds epic, right?)

---

6 Susan Weinsehenk, "Your Brain on Stories," *Psychology Today*, November 4, 2014, https://www.psychologytoday.com/us/blog/brain-wise/201411/your-brain-stories.

7 Catherine Cote, "Data Storytelling: How to Effectively Tell a Story with Data." Harvard Business School Online's "Business Insights" blog, November 23, 2021. https://online.hbs.edu/blog/post/data-storytelling.

8 Dan Roam, *The Back of the Napkin: Solving Problems and Selling Ideas with Pictures,* expanded edition (New York: Portfolio/Penguin, 2013); and *Draw to Win: A Crash Course on How to Lead, Sell, and Innovate with Your Visual Mind*, illustrated edition (New York: Portfolio/Penguin, 2016).

The Bible is chock full of real people and real events that are super amazing. There are human heroes, and not so good people, who (ironically) turn out to be heroes anyway (plot twist!). There are people we want to be like, and people we'd rather not meet in a dark alley late at night. Doesn't it make you want to find a campfire and start telling stories? Simple enough, right?

God took the time to create and pass on to us real-life stories that show us what he's like. About 55–65 percent of the Bible consists of stories!

The world of the Bible is like watching a scene taking place in the middle of *Star Wars* or *Star Trek*. It's often very different than what we are used to. And we all know (yes we do, you Sci-Fi naysayers) that we love to discover those worlds. So we need to come to the Scriptures with the attitude that the Bible is fun to discover too. Telling stories from the Bible and using stick figures to do it isn't that hard and isn't that revolutionary, but it is different. Perhaps, just perhaps, you could give it a try. And then you can be a Super Person too!

With a bit of practice, telling Jesus stories becomes easy. This amazingly nontechnical book should help you get started and get practicing. So grab a writing utensil, some paper, a friend, an enemy, a pet, and let's get started!

Which Stories Do I Tell?
Ones That Connect to People's Lives!

This is the scenario: You are having a cup of coffee with someone and they tell you about a real-life problem. You now have a chance to tell a story from the Bible. Which one do you choose? Here are some ideas to help you get started.

Problem	SOME Potential Stories
1. Financial problems	• Don't be anxious—Luke 12:22–34; Matthew 6:25–34 • Elijah, a Widow, and Miraculous Provision—1 Kings 17:7–16 • Elisha, a Widow, and Miraculous Provision—2 Kings 4:1–7 • Feeding of the five thousand—Luke 9:12–17; Matthew 14:13–21; Mark 6:30–44 • Coin in the fish's mouth—Matthew 17:24–27
2. Conflict with a loved one	• The Unmerciful Servant—Matthew 18:21–35 • Paul and Barnabas—Acts 15:36–40 • Jacob and Esau reconcile—Genesis 33:1–11 • Joseph is reconciled—Genesis 46:28–34 • The Prodigal son—Luke 15:11–32
3. Knowing how to choose a spouse	• Abraham's servant and Rebekah—Genesis 24:1–67 (The message here is to pray and do whatever the Lord tells you to do.) • Jacob and Rachel—Genesis 29:1–30 (The message here is that a good spouse is worth waiting for.) • Solomon—1 Kings 11:1–6 (The message is to marry a godly person, not to marry hundreds of other people!) • The Lord chooses David—1 Samuel 16:1–13 (The message is to pray and look on the inside—not the outside—in any selection process.)

Problem	SOME Potential Stories
4. Marriage problems/potential divorce	• Adam and Eve—Genesis 3:1–9 (Remember why marriage is hard.) • Hosea 3:1–5 (Reconciliation can be costly.) • Joseph and Mary—Matthew 1:18–25 (Are you sure you see your spouse as the Lord sees them?)
5. Not getting along with children	• Isaac reconciled with his sons—Genesis 35:27–29 • Jacob and his sons reconciled—Genesis 45:25–28 • Prodigal son—Luke 15:11–32 (Unconditional love) • Moses and the basket—Exodus 2:1–10 (Letting go) • Abraham and Isaac—Genesis 22:1–19 (Surrender your child to God.) • David and Absalom—2 Samuel 14:1–33 • Jesus and the children—Matthew 19:13–15
6. Sickness/Illness	• Jesus heals—John 9:1–6 • Peter heals—Acts 3:1–10 • Paul heals—Acts 19:11–12 • Naaman the Syrian—2 Kings 5:1–14 • Hezekiah—2 Kings 20:1–7 • Servant of the high priest—Luke 22:47–51 • Blind Bartimaeus—Mark 10:46–52; Luke 18:35–43 • Paralytic lowered—Mark 2:1–12; Luke 5:17–26
7. Recent death in family	• Mary—John 19:26–27 (Jesus understands the ramifications of death and makes provision for his mother.) • Jesus weeps at Lazarus' death—John 11:28–44 (The main point is not the raising of the dead, which does actually still happen! The main point is that Jesus grieves over death.) • Take time to grieve—Matthew 14:1–2, 12–13

Problem	SOME Potential Stories
8. Stress/too much to do	• Martha and Mary—Luke 10:38–42 • Don't be anxious—Luke 12:22–34; Matthew 6:25–34 • Four soils—Mark 4:14–20 (Danger of choking your walk) • Moses assigns leaders—Exodus 18:13–27 • Jesus calms the storm—Mark 4:35–41; Matthew 8:23–27; Luke 8:22–25 • Jesus goes away to pray—Luke 5:15–16; Matthew 14:23; Mark 1:35–38 • After a busy time of work, Jesus encourages retreat—Mark 6:30–31
9. Growing old	• Naomi is blessed in her old age—Ruth 4:13–17 • King Rehoboam's advisors—1 Kings 12:1–15 • Simeon—Luke 2:25–35 • Anna—Luke 2:36–38 • Abraham called at age 75—Genesis 12:1–4 • Abraham's child in their old age—Genesis 21:1–7 • Caleb—Joshua 14:6–15
10. Being uncertain of the future	• Jesus' friends—John 15:15–16 • Elisha and the musician—2 Kings 3:13–20 (God speaks even to people who don't like him, if they ask!) • The end is known—Revelation 21:9–27 • Don't be anxious—Luke 12:22–34; Matthew 6:25–34 • God can give dreams—Genesis 37:5–8; 40:1–23; 41:1–36 • Esther—Esther 4:1–17 • Road to Emmaus—Luke 24:13–34 • Gideon—Judges 6:33–40 • Ruth and Naomi—Ruth 4:13–17

Problem	SOME Potential Stories
11. Having trouble conceiving	• Sarah—Genesis 21:1–7 • Rachel—Genesis 30:1–24 • Elizabeth—Luke 1:5–25 • Hannah—1 Samuel 1:1–20
12. Fear about making the wrong decision at an important life juncture	• Uzziah—2 Chronicles 26:1–5 • Abraham's servant—Genesis 24:9–22 • John the Baptist—Matthew 11:2–6 • Holy Spirit—John 14:15–18 • The call of Peter—Matthew 4:18–22; Luke 5:1–11; Mark 1:16–20
13. Needing a job	• Don't be anxious—Luke 12:22–34; Matthew 6:25–34 • A father gives good gifts—Matthew 7:7–11 • Jacob's goats—Genesis 30:31–43 (God can provide in unusual ways. Pray and ask him for strategy.) • Parable of the vineyard—Matthew 20:1–16 (God can provide, even if the job comes late.) • Persistent widow—Luke 18:1–8 • Coin in the fish's mouth—Matthew 17:24–27
14. Being a good parent	• Solomon's decision – 1 Kings 3:16–28 (God revealed the good parent and took care of her. Message is to trust God and do what is right by your kids.) • Prodigal son—Luke 15:11–32 (The story is really more about being a good father.) • King Lemuel's mother—Proverbs 31:1–9 (She passes on godly wisdom to her son.) • Moses' mother—Exodus 2:1–10 (In extreme cases, still obey God. He can provide for your child.) • Job—Job 1:1–5 • Mary and Joseph—Luke 2:41–52

3 Super Non-Advanced Drawing for Non-Drawers

DON'T CUT OFF YOUR ARM!

Maybe it should be obvious that cutting off your arm is a really bad idea. (Don't even go there. Don't stop to visualize it for too long. It's gross.) Many adults, however, look at me like I'm asking them to cut off their drawing arm when I ask them to draw pictures. Sometimes people express that they think drawing pictures is childish, but more often people just know that they are bad at drawing. They start twitching and moaning when I mention drawing. (OK, that only happened once—but it was memorable!)

Those who are still trying to figure out how to get out of drawing pictures might be like me. So imagine how awkward it is for me now to be the person who is famous (in my own mind) for drawing stick figures. Well, not just stick figures, but pretty *bad* stick figures at that. (When I was asked what I wanted to be when I grew up, I didn't respond, "the really bad stick-figure lady." But these things happen. And I've accepted my title with as much grace as I can.)

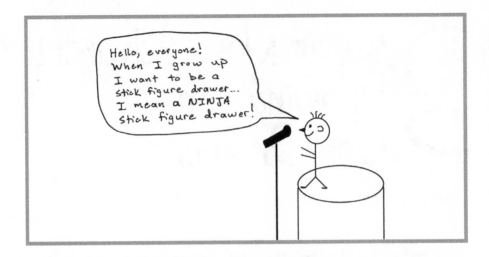

Many years ago (like five years ago, not twenty), we had a real artist in one of the trainings we run. She would spend hours drawing pictures to use in telling Jesus stories. Her pictures were nice, but no one else ever wanted to show her their pictures. They were too embarrassed, because they naturally compared their images to hers. The same thing will happen to the people that you are drawing for, if you make your pictures too fancy. They will be intimidated, and the stories won't spread easily from person to person.

So let me give *you* some pointers on drawing stick figures.

NOW THAT YOU KEPT THAT ARM, LET'S TRAIN IT!

Arms and hands are very useful for holding pens and drawing pictures and about a million other things. But like all good things, the hand must have at least a little bit of practice to be able to draw stick figures. It won't take much practice or much skill, so don't worry. You'll be just fine. And if you are an artist, Principle #1 will probably drive you crazy …

Principle #1: Your stick figures MUST be bad.

This is particularly true if you are leading the Bible study or if you are a person of authority in any form of group other than a group of local artists. (Then I have no advice for you, as I would *never* be asked to lead such a group!) If you are just drawing pictures for yourself in your own private journal, then feel free to make them look good. You can spend hours or weeks or years on them, if you are doing them for yourself or for the local museum of modern art (now that would be cool!).

The first reason for this principle is very practical. You are busy. If these things take you hours to draw, you will end up not doing it. You will hate the pictures. You will hate me. It will be very bad. Since you are busy, do some quick and dirty drawing. Well, it doesn't have to be dirty, just quick.

The second reason for this is that you might be drawing these pictures on a napkin as you go. This is a really good thing to do in a coffee shop or while visiting a friend. You have some conversation, and you end up talking about something deeper than cookies (yum!). What you are talking about reminds you of a Jesus story, so you pull out a piece of paper and start drawing pictures as you tell the story. If you take forever to draw the pictures and you slow down the story, then people will get bored. And the next time you begin to tell a Jesus story, they will zone out instead of zoning in.

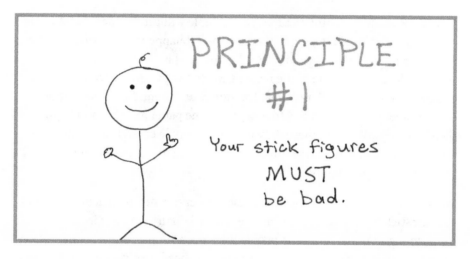

PRINCIPLE #1

Your stick figures MUST be bad.

Now this whole keeping-your-stick-figures-bad thing seems counterintuitive to a person who believes in excellence. And let me be clear, I do believe in excellence. But in this case, excellence does not lie in the direction of amazing pictures.

Excellence happens when we have what experts call "maximum reproducibility." Now anytime people get advanced degrees for stuff, long words have to be involved. But all that maximum reproducibility actually means is: *We can all do it*. Or maybe: *Anyone can do it*. Anyway, the point is that this whole drawing pictures thing is not only for the "true arteests" among us. It's also for the rest of us, who aren't sure which colors are primary and which are just ugly. So we have to make it simple enough that we can all be part of it.

If we draw really beautiful pictures, then people will get the idea that drawing pictures is only for some people. And when that happens, we slow down the ability for Jesus stories to go viral. And going viral is what we want when it comes to Jesus news. One of the reasons we do the pictures is so that people can have a visual reminder of what the stories are about. But if the stories are complicated, people won't feel free to grab some paper at home and begin their drawings. We want these drawings to be simple enough that when these individuals are in their next boring board meeting, their margin doodles will turn into Jesus stick figures.

So now we begin the amazing and awesome step-by-step instructions on how to draw stick figures. The first example is a stick figure in about its simplest form, though I have seen some people draw even simpler ones. I usually draw a stick figure in five easy steps. I begin with the head. Beginning with the head has the advantage that I can erase or scratch out the head and try again when the head looks too blobby or like it was recently in a catastrophic car accident. This often happens to me, as I have a hard time holding my hand steady. So most of my poor people just don't look too good. I'm busy and can't be too worried about the perfect symmetry of the stick-figure heads.

The rest is pretty standard stick-figure stuff. Lots of sticks here and there to make a body and arms and legs. Then a smiley face. If I'm being really *avant-garde* (notice the use of French to make you feel artistic), I might add a nose or ears or even some hair, but all of those things are optional. Sometimes I go all out and add shoes or feet or even a hand. Hands are hard. I try to avoid drawing hands, but sometimes people in the story are holding something and you really need them. (I should point out that *VeggieTales* did just fine without ever including any hands, and if it's good enough for them, then it's surely good enough for you and me!) You'll see some drawings of hands throughout this book. They are mostly sticks on sticks, and that's good enough.

Don't forget noses. Ears are sometimes nice too!

Now that you have studied these amazing step-by-step directions for drawing stick figures, did you notice all the advanced techniques that are used? You didn't? That's right! Doing it right means doing it so simply that you are laughing with the ridiculousness of the drawings. And no one—I repeat, no one—reading this book will ever think, "There is no way I can do that!" No, even the youngest person, who perhaps has never even held a pencil, is thinking, "Seriously?! I can totally outdo that!" If that is what you also are thinking, then the drawing was done correctly. If you feel intimidated in any way whatsoever, then the drawings are not achieving their aim.

Now suppose you do want to be a teensy bit advanced, you might take the body shape and fill it out a bit. For example, you could use a square or a circle or a triangle as the body of the stick figure. This has the advantage that you can put a symbol in there so that people will know one character from another in your pictures. It also means that women are more easily distinguishable than men and that certain characters can be known by their shape. One guy might be a square while another one is a rectangle. Still easy and totally reproducible, but it gives a bit of *panache* (More French! Are you feeling artsy yet?) to your drawings, while still maintaining maximum reproducibility.

But, if Paul or Peter or Lydia or Cornelius or Moses or whomever looks different, then be consistent and let each one of them look a bit different. See if you can tell who the following drawings represent.

That's Peter or Paul, Lydia, and Cornelius. Do you see how they are each different and yet still easy to draw? Hopefully you don't think the bar has been raised too high for you.

This might be a good place to talk about being consistent in drawing Jesus. A lot of people like to put a sash on Jesus. (Talk about raising the bar!) This looks regal in many cultures around the world and has caught on as a result.

As for me, I always make sure that Jesus has a beard. Well, except when I am in Myanmar. In Myanmar, we found out that only Muslims have beards. So when Jesus had a beard, people said, "We had no idea Jesus was Muslim!" Well, that didn't work, now did it? So we should leave off the beard when in Myanmar. (Have you been sure to leave off the beard every single time you have been in Myanmar? I hope so!) This highlights an important principle: *Test how you draw your pictures if you are going to use them cross-culturally.*

Stick figures seem to work pretty well across cultures in general. Many, many missionaries have had a chance to test them out over time. Still, always be sure to double-check with a trusted local friend before you start using your stick figures widely, if you are telling Jesus stories in a culture that is not your own. (Wouldn't it be awesome if we all did that?)

Jesus, as an advanced stick figure, might look like the following drawing in which he has *both* a beard *and* a sash. (Wow!)

If I've done it correctly (and I declare that I have!), then Jesus is more recognizable, but you still don't feel like he is so advanced that you cannot draw him yourself. Maybe you think he looks too this or too that. The good news is that there are no physical descriptions of Jesus in the Bible. So you can draw him however you want. He can be any color or any size.

Just a note to those of you who are planning to share Jesus with Muslims. In some few places in the Muslim world, the people do not want there to be any images of God or the Prophet Muhammad. In general, Jesus is exempt from this rule, since they don't consider Jesus to be God. Still, once again, it would be wise to check with a trusted local friend before getting too gung ho about showing your drawings publicly. Such pictures have been used in many places in the Muslim world, and can likely be used wherever you might happen to go, but check first!

This leads us to our next amazing principle …

Principle #2: Your stick figures MUST be consistent.

If Jesus looks one way in your first drawing, he needs to look that way in all your drawings. If you don't like how a character ends up looking (your drawing is ugly or doesn't seem right), you can change it in the next story, but you'll be stuck with that terrible stick figure for the course of that one story at least. (Unless you dramatically crumple up your paper and start over, of course. But I advise against doing that too often. Life is short, and you are probably busy.)

This consistency helps people recognize the characters more easily. So if you draw Paul one way at the beginning of your story, keep drawing him that way throughout your entire story. For some reason, in my imagination Paul is often bald, so I draw him that way. I put a dollar sign on Zacchaeus, so people can easily recognize him. In my mind, Mary, the mother of Jesus, has long hair. The point is that no matter how you draw these people, draw them the same way every time. There are no physical descriptions of any of these people in the Bible, so you can draw them in any way that seems right to you. However, once you pick a way, stick to that way.

This leads us to our next amazing principle …

Principle #3: If you can use color, you should.

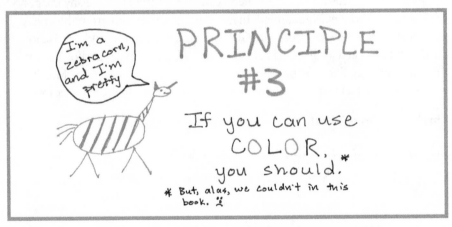

Colors help people remember and are just more fun and generally more pleasing. Once again, however, the most important measure of success is *maximum reproducibility*. If you go someplace where people are very poor and can't really afford lots of colors, then you should be sure to use only one color. This way people won't think that they need to go get lots of pens or markers or whatever to be able to tell the stories.

If you use a set of colorful markers to tell Jesus stories, but the locals can't afford to buy them on their own, then you have violated *maximum reproducibility*. Likewise, if you bring fancy notebooks from home as gifts for the people, you have also violated *maximum reproducibility*. You might think markers and notebooks aren't too expensive, and you would be happy to provide them for people—in which case your dream for the worship of Jesus might be too small.

Will you buy notebooks and markers for the literally thousands of people who will begin to worship Jesus and tell Jesus stories? Likely not. As soon as you leave or the money runs out, the local people will say, "We can't afford the colors and the paper, so we cannot tell Jesus stories." Be sure to use whatever is available and affordable in the local environment.

Even if you are visiting a relatively wealthy nation or region, be aware that there might be poorer families in your midst. Perhaps they don't have good jobs or perhaps they are refugees or immigrants.

Conversely, in some wealthy countries in which we have drawn Jesus stick figures, the locals asked me, "We *never* have paper and pen with us, but we all have an iPad. Can we draw our pictures on an iPad?" After I checked to make sure it was true, we all started drawing on iPads. As Bob Dylan famously wrote and sang in 1964, "The times they are a-changin'." Some kids today can make their own very sophisticated comic books and animated characters. If you are working in a place like that and the kids (and maybe adults too!) like to do those sorts of things, then let them. Personally, I also make them practice the old-fashioned way and explain that they need to be aware of poorer people too.

Likewise, you don't want to think things like, "I could draw pictures and tell this story, but I only have this one stupid pen." Such thinking is definitely bad. In fact, if you don't have a pen, you should be able to draw in dust, in dirt, in sand, or on a dirty car. Ask the person next to you for a pen, if needed, and grab a napkin (that's a *serviette* to my more Frenchy English-speaking friends!). In some places, we have gone dumpster-diving to find something we could draw on. We found old books and drew in the margins. We found wrappers and even leaves, in some cases. Be creative!

Over the years, I have found myself wondering things like: How do I draw a person walking? How do I draw a person sitting? How do I draw a person baptizing someone? When these questions arise, I act out the motion I wish to draw and then notice what position my body is in. I then try to imitate that on the page—sometimes successfully, sometimes not. The person in my pictures who is baptizing another person still looks like they are drowning them! But actual baptisms sometimes look that way too (unless you know what's going on, of course).

Usually, if I think about it for a couple of seconds, I can figure out how to make a leg or an arm bend to look like action. So I'm confident that you will be able to act out a motion and get a feel for how to create motion in your pictures as well. If all else fails, draw an arrow, which usually helps people figure out that something is in motion.

Sadly, people are not the only things that we will need drawn. There will be all sorts of animals and buildings and houses and mountains and all sorts of normal, everyday, generally pesky things that I don't know how to draw. (Why can't people confine their stories to the things I'm able to draw?) All animals have a tendency to look alike when I draw them. I do *try* to make the pigs distinguishable from the cows, but I'm not always successful. Here are my animals. Can you tell which is which?

I'm going to guess that you feel like you could draw animals at least as nice as those. And remember, don't be too tempted to make your pictures really good, except maybe for your own pleasure in your own notebook. Otherwise people will feel that they can't draw pictures. Also, if your pictures are taking you too long to draw, you will quit doing it because it will be too much trouble. So keep it simple. Trees, mountains, etc., are pretty much the same now as they were when I was in kindergarten, so I think you can imagine what those would look like, and I will save my ego a bit and not draw them here.

The most difficult thing to draw is God the Father. Even the Holy Spirit is easier to draw than God the Father is! (Think wind symbols!) The problem is that God the Father is so "I am what I am" that we aren't sure about the best way to draw him. He is so holy and so awesome and so wonderful that anything we draw is a poor reflection of who he is.

I have not yet settled on a good way to draw God the Father. I sometimes draw him as a burning bush, but then it doesn't seem right to do it that way every time. Sometimes he becomes eyes looking on, but that doesn't quite seem right either. He is intensely personal, our Heavenly Father, so sometimes I just want to draw him as a person, but that doesn't seem quite right either. So, if and when you get it figured out, you let me know. For now, I have a tendency to draw him a bit like a personified cloud with lightning coming out, but I'm always scared that a *real* theologian will come along and see that and scoff at me.

I have a friend much smarter than me (shocking, but true!), and she usually uses a triangle to draw God the Father. That also helps her explain deep concepts like the Trinity too. (For the super-theologians among us, we all know that *any* explanation of the Trinity is inadequate, but this gets us in the ballpark! And they have cookies in ballparks, so that's a good place to be!) So I've stolen that from her. Here are some ways I have drawn God the Father.

This might be a good time to point out that people and God are not always happy. (I'm sure that was a shocker!) I can make people look happy, sad, or mad. Beyond that, I'm afraid that expressions don't get too complex in my drawings.

There are a surprising number of scenes in the Bible in which big crowds are present. I have to say that I did not notice this until I started to draw pictures. And when I discovered it, I usually thought, "There is no way I am drawing thousands of people into this picture" … and then threw my pen down and went to get cookies with ice cream. Now I often draw crowds as either body-less heads or sometimes simply as X's. But don't leave them out! If they are in the story, they are important. In fact, you might begin to realize how often Jesus had a crowd watching him, and how strategic he really was.

UPPING YOUR GAME

Some of you are into the stick figures, and you'd like to learn to do it better. That's fine, as long as you don't get too fancy. Because what happens if you do? That's right, you lose maximum reproducibility. None of the resources below are necessary, but some readers will want more help and guidance. So here are a couple of items that might interest you.

If you'd really like to learn to draw better and more simply? Ed Emberley's *Drawing Book: Make a World* is amazing. It is awesomely simple and fun. Ed does a good job of showing how to position stick figures in different poses. His drawings are dots and lines and geometric shapes. Easy-peasy, reproducible, and fun.

(Can I let you in on a secret? Ed Emberley inspired me to put the disciples on an Italian gondola and also a pirate boat in my own private and secret journals. He showed me how to draw them, and it was fun. I know the disciples were never on a gondola or a pirate ship, but for my own journal, it's fine. Now be sure not to tell anyone, OK?)

And if you must, cheat and look things up on the internet (if you have it). Then copy *their* pictures! I have found this useful if I am trying to draw something very abstract, like righteousness. The website called TheNounProject.com has simple icons of all sorts of things. The artists there often give me some ideas on how to picture something. I can usually take it from there and simplify it enough to be usable and reproducible for all. Their drawings might help you too!

Discovery Bible Studies

The really astute may have noticed that there is no traditional teaching time in the Bible studies or church meetings outlined here. That is, there is no time when someone stands up and explains the Bible passage being studied. This is deliberate and by design. Those who are familiar with traditional teaching methods may find this hard to wrap their minds around, but give it a try! It really does work.

When people work together to learn a passage from the Bible, the Holy Spirit is an amazing teacher. He can be trusted to highlight parts of the text. When people learn directly from the Holy Spirit in community, the teaching has a tendency to stick better and be remembered. Also, when people are involved in the process of learning, they will remember better too. This is because being involved in the process involves thinking. Thinking is good.

Different people have different ways of doing Discovery Bible Study (DBS), but the core of it is the same: Read the text and ask questions of the group. Let the answers percolate up from the group. Here I have offered the absolute simplest form of Discovery Bible Study with only three key questions that are asked of every passage in the Bible:

1. What do you learn about God/Jesus/Holy Spirit?

2. What do you learn about humans/us?

3. What should we do about it? OR How should we live differently as a result of this teaching? OR Which of the seven commands (see p. 70) can we grow in?

Most DBS facilitators will end up asking more questions than just these three core questions. For example:

1. Did anyone else also see that?

2. Any comments on that?

3. Where is that in the story?

4. What part of the story made you think of that?

5. Anyone else want to share?

6. Can you think of any other ways we can live this out?

7. Maybe that is hard for us to do. How can we begin?

DBS facilitators will also often say things like:

1. Oh, good, I like that.

2. Wow!

3. Awesome!

4. I hadn't thought of that!

5. Good stuff.

6. Well said.

7. Thanks for sharing.

People often have certain fears about this method. Let's examine some of them here:

1. People will go off into heresy

Sometimes this happens, but not as often as you might think. If someone says something that is clearly wrong, usually the facilitator can wait a second to see if someone else in the group will correct it. This often happens. If not, the facilitator can say, "Where do you see that in the text?" Often, there is a link to the text in the mind of the disciple. It's just that the facilitator didn't see it. And sometimes the facilitator has to say, "I know it might look like that here, but there are other parts of the Bible we haven't gotten to yet. Let me give you a sneak peek." Young facilitators who don't have much Bible knowledge themselves are taught to ask, "Is that in the text?" This clears up the vast majority of problems pretty quickly.

2. People will say too much

This usually happens when one person is not very socially aware or has a dominant personality. If this is the case, the facilitator might have to say, "Your insights are always really good, but let's give someone else a chance to speak up." This will solve most problems. If not, then the facilitator may have to have a side conversation with the person who is talking too much. Sometimes the culture is an issue here, and facilitators will have to examine relationships between older and younger and male and female to see if those issues are also at play.

3. People will not say enough

This usually happens when people are worried about getting the answers wrong or if they don't yet know each other well. The people in some cultures are not used to thinking on their own, either. If people are too shy to say their answers out loud, then let them first whisper their answers into the ear of the facilitator. The facilitator can then let them know that is a good answer before they say it in front of the whole group.

4. People will lack enough information to truly understand

This can happen with some difficult passages, but it is less common than one might think. If so, then provide the background knowledge you feel is necessary before you tell the story the first time. Keep it short. Simply provide enough information to understand the passage you are studying.

Many believers know that Christ should be shared, but too often they don't apply that call to themselves. Telling them your reasoning in your opening explanation should spark something in them. OK, it's time to tell the story to the group. At last!

4 Becoming a Story Ninja

CRAFTING IS OLD-SCHOOL, BUT BEING A NINJA IS *REALLY* OLD-SCHOOL

Ninjas are even more old-school than spinning wheels, but somehow one of them is cool and the other is not.

Unfortunately, for most craftsmen, when people hear the word *craft*, they think of old-fashioned things that people actually just don't want anymore. Happily, this is changing now, as people are "re-discovering" that it's actually really awesome when you receive a gift that someone made specifically for you with their own little hands. Or even better is when we get to use our own little hands to make a gift for someone else. Even then, to try to regain some popularity, the term for making-stuff-with-your-own-hands has had to change from being a "crafter" to being a "maker."

COWABUNGA!

STORY NINJAS

craft...

make.....

EXCEL!!

Since the common term of *crafting* might make you yawn if you haven't yet been properly enlightened (and yawns are contagious, so stop it!), this book will use the totally exciting, captivating, amazing term *Story Ninja* to identify ourselves. It's likely true that everyone thinks that being a ninja is cool, even if you also use or own a spinning wheel.

According to good ol' Google, a ninja is "a person who excels in a particular skill or activity." Were you expecting something different? Maybe something to do with assassins and spying? Well, yes, that is a definition of ninja too, but this book cannot make you good at being a spy or an assassin. (I want to go on the record here to say that if you love Jesus, you probably shouldn't be an assassin. Just sayin'.)

Some people just naturally tell stories well—they are born Story Ninjas. They are probably the center of attention of family get-togethers, at parties, and standing around the really weak coffee they offer at most churches. If you are that person, then I give you permission to skip this section. (Does she really keep telling us we can skip parts of this book? Amazing!) However, almost everyone, including already good storytellers, get better if they prepare and practice their stories. Very few Story Ninjas are just born. Most practice, and you likely should too.

Story Ninjas keep their stories lively and interesting, neither too long nor too short for the setting. Everyone knows what happens to the long-winded uncle at the family gathering who always tells the same story over and over again. Everyone avoids him! On the other hand, the nearly silent aunt who provides no details and monosyllabic answers also gets avoided due to the long, awkward silences. Story Ninjas can avoid being either one of those people with some practice and preparation.

NINJA TOOLS

The first tool of a Story Ninja is a bow and arrow. Stories should fly straight and true and hit their mark.

Story Ninja Tool #1 The Bow and Arrow—Make sure stories fly straight and hit their mark.

Full disclosure here: Sometimes people talk about topics that they don't a clue about. In fact, I might be about to talk about a bow and arrow as if I have a clue, maybe. As long as one has seen these things done on TV or in movies, then it's OK, right? Because one thing that anyone who has seen a bow and arrow in a movie (or maybe even real life) will notice is that all of those bow-and-arrow people seem to aim carefully before they release their weapon. This is probably generally appreciated by the people in their vicinity who don't want to be hit by an arrow. Friendly fire is never a good thing.

Therefore, it seems surprising that people release their stories into the ether without having any idea at all where the story is going, or even what its point might be. Stories should always have a point to them. They might be funny, heartwarming, dramatic, long, or short. However, all stories have as their target the human heart that is receiving and telling the story. (Yes, even the teller is transformed and changed in the process of the telling. Doesn't that make you even more excited about being a Story Ninja?)

However, storytelling is not only about the needs of the storyteller. No, storytelling is an inherently communal activity. In other words, it takes two to tell a story: one to speak and one to listen. A Story Ninja's goal is to connect to other human hearts to build up, encourage, edify, lift up, inform, educate, connect, empathize, and a whole host of other wonderful things.

It's hard to do those things if the Story Ninjas aren't quite clear on the main point of their story. If they aren't clear on the main point, then they might ramble or include irrelevant details. When people aren't sure why they are telling a story or about the needs of the hearers, they usually ramble, and their stories get too long.

Story Ninja Tool #2 A Map—Show (or even announce!) step-by-step how to arrive at a destination.

Not everyone has a good idea of what makes a great story. This leads to the next Ninja tool, a map. Once a ninja has figured out where they are and where they need to be, then a map will show them how to get there. In the past, maps required some skill to use. Now GPS maps do all the work for people. It would be really awesome if we had a GPS map for stories, but NINJAS DID NOT HAVE GPS!!! So old-school, here we come.

The following framework represents the ninja map that will help to make sure that the story is getting to where it needs to go. (Note: Do *not* check out just because this map sort of reminds you of a high school English class. It might look similar, but maybe—just maybe—they were teaching something useful in that class. Now there's a thought. Sometimes you get permission to skip parts of this book, and sometimes you don't!)

1. Beginning—In the beginning of a story, things are usually good. No evil person has taken over the world. No problems have presented themselves. Things are good and happy. This is also where the Story Ninja will usually tell who is in the story and where the story takes place.

2. Middle—Something happens to break up the happiness. Things get bad, sometimes very bad. There are problems. There's lots of tension, concern, conflict, and maybe even fear.

3. Climax—Something really scary, interesting, dramatic, or wonderful happens and the problem gets solved. This could involve lots of chasing in a modern movie (too much chasing—just get on with the plot!). Or it might involve working out relationships, undergoing a successful surgery, or a miraculous God-intervention.

4. End—Things are good again, or at least at a steady state. Circumstances are usually resolved and worked out. In very happy stories, things are usually better at the end than they were at the beginning. In real life, we might not know the end yet. So we have to tell a pre-ending, where we can see God working or feel his peace.

This mapping system is already present in Bible stories (it's a very well-crafted book!), so when telling stories from the Bible, you won't need to access this map too much. However, some stories are very long (e.g., Moses, Joseph) and will need to be compressed. In the case of shortening a story from the Bible, this map is very helpful. More on crafting biblical stories below. ...

If you are unsure whether or not a story is a good story, start with the problem. Start in the middle with what has gone wrong. This will help you focus on the really interesting part of the story. Sometimes I like to test up-and-coming Story Ninjas with a quiz. I'll say, "Quick, tell me a story!" Then they sometimes say things like:

- Yesterday we went to the store.
- We got some groceries.
- We came home.

Well, that's nice, but it's *boring*. So boring! Where is the drama, the action, the excitement, the problem? Now let's try again:

- Yesterday we went to the store to get ready for the blizzard. (Problem #1: Blizzard. Blizzards are scary. We could die.)
- We went to get carrots, but they were all out of organic carrots. (Problem #2: No organic carrots! We'll surely starve!)
- We debated about buying the regular, nonorganic carrots. (Gasp! No! Don't do it. How will they solve the problem?)
- But then we saw one bag of organic baby carrots. (Hurray! Problem solved.)

- We grabbed them just before a whole bunch of other people came in. (Climax. Happy dance. Too bad for those other people, eh? We were sure those other people were also after organic carrots to help them survive the blizzard!)

- So we knew we wouldn't die in the blizzard because we'd have organic carrots to see us through.
(The end. Things are good again.)

The second story is much more interesting because there is a problem in the middle of it. It's made even more interesting (I hope!) because the problem (lack of organic carrots) does not fit the setting of the story. (I'm pretty sure people can survive an impending blizzard without organic carrots.) *When in doubt about your ability to be a Story Ninja, start with the problem, which will center the rest of the story, and then work your way back from there.*

PERSONAL NINJA STORIES

Story Ninja Tool #3 Our Testimonies—Our personal Jesus stories are powerful.

Every Story Ninja has stories that have happened in their own lives. In church or in the Bible, these kinds of stories are also called testimonies. These personal Jesus stories are often shared in casual conversations, particularly with people who are not yet believers. The stories (and the Ninjas who tell them) are usually unassuming, simple, and true.

Such stories are typically easy to tell since there is firsthand experience of the events. These autobiographical events are generally very powerful and Ninja-like. They often intervene in the midst of relationships and transform the mundane into a holy moment. These tales will often set up shop and begin percolating in someone's heart. Because they are personal, true events, they are not usually rejected and are well remembered.

Testimonies are one of the most powerful tools in the Story Ninja's toolbox. Personal Jesus stories, known as testimonies, should be told in every workplace, coffee shop, store, bus, etc., every day by all the Jesus people of the world, young and old! God told us to keep his words in our hearts, and to "Repeat them again and again to your children. Talk about them when you are at home and when you are on the road, when you are going to bed and when you are getting up" (Deut 6:7).

So, yes, the Lord might have just given you permission to tell that *same* story of when God came through for you (and God's people) to your kids over and over again, no matter how much they roll their eyes! However, the main point here is that *all* believers are commanded to talk about Jesus wherever we are and at all times of the night and day.

It is important to differentiate this tool of storytelling and testimony from a different tool. Sometimes people confuse the personal testimony tool with the preaching tool. Preaching is not bad; in fact, a good number of people are paid to preach for a living, while others are invited to preach as a gift to a church community. However, preaching during coffee break at work is not usually welcome.

Preaching can sometimes be called exposition. Neither one of them is storytelling. It's surprising how often people begin to tell a story and then end up preaching instead. Let's imagine two human beings are hanging out. They are doing whatever it is they do for fun: working on the spinning wheel, jogging, hanging out on the beach, etc. Their conversation goes past cookie level (yum!), and the Story Ninja reaches out to the other person. The Story Ninja says, "How are things going at work? How are you and your spouse? How are the kids?"

Naturally, the Story Ninja does not just have all of these questions roll off of their tongue in a sequence. The Story Ninja does have some basic social skills, after all! The idea is that Story Ninjas are people who care and love, and so they will ask others about their lives. After asking, Story Ninjas are good listeners, to both the other person and to the Holy Spirit. Otherwise they will not know best how to help or encourage their friend.

In due time, the friend begins to open up about a problem at work. After listening attentively and giving the Holy Spirit some time to speak to their hearts too, the friend (who is clearly not a Story Ninja yet!) says, "You need to pray more. There are several main ways that people can petition God. They can engage in intercessory prayer, fast, worship, participate in corporate prayer meetings, or even journal. Each one of these has several advantages and disadvantages. ..."

That's not bad or wrong per se. It's all true. And it's almost always true that someone could pray more. But it's not a story, it's not interesting, and it's not likely to be well received or to be implemented. Maybe, but not likely.

On the other hand, a Story Ninja might say, "Several weeks ago my church had two weeks of special prayer. I went there and put my one prayer request on the wall: to find the time and space to write a book for work. I had been trying to find the time for months, and I had even blown a deadline. I *hate* blowing deadlines, so it was really bothering me. Every morning I would walk and walk and ask God to show me the solution. Sometimes I'd get no real peace out of the prayer time, truthfully. But I just kept asking God to provide a solution and then help me to recognize the solution when he did. Then finally, about two weeks after the prayer time at church, my family just opened up time and space for me to go away and work on that book. That little house I went to was perfect, and now that book is written. I just didn't see any way to make it happen, and God just suddenly provided a way through my family." (That just might be a true story … Wink, wink.)

This story follows the course laid out on the map. But before going to the map, Story Ninjas have to decide where to aim the Ninja Arrow. The point of this story is to build up and encourage a friend who is struggling in terms of their work. So anything that will not help build them up need not be included. Also, most friends have a fairly short attention span, and it's not good to dominate conversation. So this story should be short. (Ninjas have to sneak in and out quickly!)

1. Beginning—It's only implied in this story. Since our stories have to be short, sometimes we just imply that there was a time before this problem, but jump right into the problem.

2. Middle—Problem: The need to write a book, but no time or place to do it.

3. Climax—The person telling the story tries prayer time at church and personal prayer times repeatedly.

4. End—The problem was finally resolved through family. The book got written.

In this second example, because it is a story, the brain will awaken and become involved in the story. The body will likely actually even release chemicals that will help build a bond between the two people. As a result, the listener is much more likely to actually implement the suggested solutions (praying at church, personal prayer, and waiting on God) than they would be in the earlier preaching exposition. Nearly the same suggestions were made in both instances, but the story sneaks in there and easily builds up the other person by building empathy.

BIBLICAL NINJA STORIES

The Bible is full of amazing real-life tales! In fact, roughly 55–65 percent of the Bible consists of stories.[9] The other 35 percent of the Bible consists of letters, poems, prophetic words, and whatever you want to call the book of Revelation (and some parts of Daniel and Ezekiel). Despite the Bible being incredibly story-oriented, it seems that many modern Christians are biased toward the other 35 percent of the Bible. Most contemporary Jesus followers are better able to quote something from Paul's letters or the Psalms than to retell any of Jesus' parables or any historical happenings.

Memorizing parts of the Bible is a good idea. In fact, being able to quote Paul or the Psalms or some of the sayings of Jesus is *really* good. Too few people today bother to memorize anything. It does seem that old-school ninjas were probably good at memorizing things.

If you have a regular pattern of memorizing Scripture—then good job, keep it up, and encourage others to do it too! Memorized portions of Scripture can pop into hearts and minds in the midst of any other activities we are doing. Children can memorize a lot of Scripture, and families can memorize the Bible together.

However, memorization is not one of the tools that Story Ninjas must have. Most people find memorizing whole stories too hard, and then there just wouldn't be enough Story Ninjas out there to let everyone have a chance to hear about Jesus. It's one thing to memorize a verse of the Bible. It's quite another to memorize whole stories. Instead, Story Ninjas can use the map

---

9 Tom Steffen, "Story in Life, Ministry, and Academics," Biola University Center for Christianity, Culture and the Arts. https://ccca.biola.edu/resources/2014/apr/1/story-life-ministry-and-academics/.

shown here, look at biblical drama, and tell those events in their own words. Ninjas will stay as faithful as they can to the original text, but they don't need to memorize the stories word for word.

I also don't have to memorize Bible stories word for word?

DOUBLE COWABUNGA!!

I do promise to practice, so I can be the BEST Story Ninja ever!

WOO HOO!

Memorization actually violates the principle of *maximum reproducibility*. If all of the stories have to be memorized, then most people will simply give up and tell no stories at all. They will wrongly assume that they don't have the needed skills, time, or patience. Also, when telling biblical stories in an informal setting, there probably won't be time to tell the whole story. A summary of the most relevant part of the story will have to be told instead. In fact, the whole story might switch to a headline version of that story. If people seem interested in hearing more, you can tell more later. This is where you can watch to see whether or not they lean in. And switching over to a memorized story while sitting with your friend in a canoe would probably be awkward anyway.

Let's imagine two people are hanging out together again. They have happily eaten cookies and ice cream, are in their baggy pants as a result, and are enjoying each other's company. One of them (your friend who is not yet a follower of Jesus) says, "You are always talking about God, but doesn't he just want to kill and condemn people? What's all this stuff about hell you all are always talking about?"

The Story Ninja pauses to check in with the Holy Spirit, and then says, "That's a great question. It reminds me of a man who lived a long, long time ago. His people were being treated bad—I mean, really bad, like Hitler bad— by this other group of people. So he just wanted God to strike them down and wipe them off the face of the earth. Instead, do you know what God did? He sent that man into the middle of all those bad guys and told him to tell those bad guys that they had to follow God or be wiped off the face of the earth. He was hoping that they would be killed right then, but then those really bad guys decided to follow God! And do you know how the man reacted? He was mad! Mad that God didn't just kill them all. God told the man that not only did he not want to kill those bad guys, but that he would show mercy to anyone he wanted. In the end, that man accepted God's mercy too. It's a true story."

Did you recognize the story? It is from the Bible. It's the story of Jonah and the city of Nineveh from the book of Jonah.

It would have been possible for the Story Ninja to quote 2 Peter 3:9: "The Lord isn't really being slow about his promise, as some people think. No, he is being patient for your sake. He does not want anyone to be destroyed but wants everyone to repent." That's a great piece of Scripture, one well worth memorizing. But in this context, it wouldn't have had the strength or impact of the story.

There are also several New Testament stories that would be wonderful to tell in this setting:

- Jesus accepts Zacchaeus, a notorious tax collector—Luke 19:1–10
- Jesus accepts a sinful woman who anoints his feet—Luke 7:36–50
- Jesus refuses to condemn a woman caught in adultery—John 8:1–11

There are likely many, many other stories that could also be told. However, the Story Ninja chose to go outside the normal stories she already knew. She chose to challenge herself to learn more stories and also to help broaden the stories she could pull from. The Old Testament has many wonderful stories that are rarely told, simply because believers don't think of them.

However, this telling of the story of Jonah is admittedly unusual to someone who has been a Christian for a long time. For example, the Story Ninja didn't mention the names of Jonah or Nineveh. This was done because this is an informal setting and the Story Ninja felt that the names would be unfamiliar and confusing to the hearer (who doesn't know the Bible). Giving a description of the nature of each character in the story in a way that the other person could understand seemed more in keeping with finding the mark with the arrow.

Tool 1—The Arrow—What is the point of this story?

The point is to help a friend know that God is merciful and kind. This point can be made without a big fish. Also, the big fish part is not the main point of the story here. The main point is that God showed really, really bad people great mercy and let them enter into his kingdom—and that a religious person didn't like that. So the big fish gets nixed, at least for this telling. Today a big fish would be a distraction. The main goal is to show that God invited Nineveh to repent. Also, the words *Jonah, Nineveh,* and *repent* might be confusing to the listener, so the Story Ninja opted to leave out those details.

Tool 2—The Map—Are the stages of a story present?

1. Beginning—The background to the story are filled in, but things are not good. Things are already bad at the beginning of the story. But the man is happy, since he thinks God will wipe the bad guys off the face of the earth.

2. Middle—God sends the man to tell them to follow God. They do.

3. Climax—The man is super mad and unhappy because God didn't kill them all.

4. End—The man and the and all the bad people accept God's mercy. Story Ninja puts in a little reminder at the end, just for emphasis, that this is a true story.

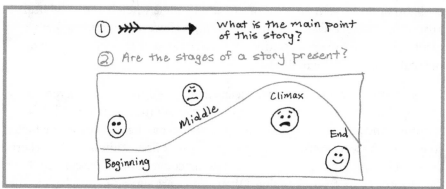

Story Ninja did a good job of getting in the basic elements of a biblical story while wearing her post-ice-cream-eating-time casual pants and hanging out with her friend. But what if there isn't even enough time to tell the one-paragraph version of the story? What if there is only enough time or interest enough for a very brief story?

This time, Story Ninja is in the break room at work. One of her colleagues says, "Christians are always just condemning people to hell. Why don't they back off?"

Story Ninja pauses for just a second and prays. Then she says, "Yeah, some people just don't get it, do they? Reminds me of a guy I read about who went and told this whole city to change their ways and turn to God. He didn't want to give this message to these evil people, but God told him he had to do it. You know what? The whole city did—the whole city! Then that guy got mad because God had been super-merciful to them. That guy was evidently hoping they'd all just die. Crazy how some people just can't see God as forgiving and kind."

Story Ninja has shortened the story even more. She has also transitioned into and out of the story with giving some agreeing statements to her colleague. She didn't defend the fact that hell exists or that repentance is necessary. Hopefully, she just gave her colleague a very short story to help her think.

Story Ninja also can't just say, "Oh yeah, that reminds of Jonah." Actually, Story Ninja could say that to someone who knows the Bible, but she can't assume that people at work have any biblical knowledge. What little bits she can pass on at work might be the only bits of the Bible that people ever get.

Story-crafting helps us to know what parts of the story ought to be simplified, shortened, or even left out. It all has to do with who the audience is and what the main point is that we are trying to make—where the arrow needs to land. This simplifying of the story is often necessary when we are sharing biblical stories in informal settings. Less of this will be done when learning biblical stories in a church meeting or in Bible studies. However, it's critical that we adapt Bible stories in social settings. Otherwise people may never get to hear any of the stories of the Bible at all.

Adapting stories in social settings means that sometimes we don't even let people know right off the bat that the stories are from the Bible. This is because many people have emotional or spiritual barriers related to the Bible. To get past those barriers, we can share the stories first, without telling where the stories came from. Then, in our follow-up conversations, we can tell them that the stories are from the Bible. Often people are surprised by what's in the Bible. But, sometimes, if we tell them initially that we are about to tell them a Bible story, they will turn off their brains before we even tell the story and will not hear it. So, sometimes it's better to tell the story first and then follow up with where the story came from later. How does the Story Ninja know when to tell from the beginning that a story is from the Bible or whether he/she should wait until later? Story Ninjas pray, try to hear instructions from the Holy Spirit, and then do their best to follow them. There is no one hard and fast rule. (Later, when we study more formal Bible storying, people will always know up front that the story is from the Bible.)

Sometimes people think that they can't share stories from the Bible in social settings. They think that such stories are off-limits. And given how they typically imagine their presentation, it would be at least socially awkward and maybe an etiquette violation. They usually seem to imagine that they are suddenly very formal and quoting the Bible word for word and then preaching about what the story means.

Hopefully Story Ninjas can now begin to have the skill to introduce biblical stories naturally, within the flow of normal life. To the extent that we never talk about Jesus in key relationships, then those people will never truly know us. It creates a false basis of relationship that lacks authenticity. However, if believers share real stories but allow others to decide not to follow Jesus—if that's the decision they choose to make—then that is truly "unconditional love." Never talking about Jesus is not love; it's indifference, isolation, and inauthenticity.

What Are the Seven Commands of Jesus?

The seven general commands of Jesus form a handy tool that helps guide us to which stories to tell and when. They are not meant to be everything a person ever needs to know about Jesus. (No need to set impossible goals, now!) They are simply a summary tool. They make things easy to remember, which is good. They also provide a path to walk along toward Jesus.

Jesus said that if we love him, we will obey his commands (John 14:15). A lot of people these days are afraid of words like *obedience*. Some have been spiritually abused or under bad leadership. Stressing obedience can be oppressive if grace is not also stressed. Obedience is a good thing because Jesus said it's a good thing.

God's Word says that his grace is abundant (1 Tim 1:14; Rom 5:17; 2 Cor 4:15; 12:9). We should celebrate attempts to be obedient, even if the attempts ultimately turn out to be failures. Likewise, the Bible tells us to confess our sins to each other (Jas 5:16). In fact, the Bible even links such confession to healing (which we all need).

When people in our church meetings confess really horrible sins (which is what *all* sin is), we should say, "Thank you so much for sharing that with us. It's such an honor to be trusted with your heart. We're sure you are grieving about the sin, since you are sharing it with us. How can we help you to not sin again?" That's obedience combined with abundant grace.

Some people have been so hurt that the mere word *obedience* turns them off. A really smart friend of mine who has a heart for broken people talks about "Seven Experiences with Jesus" instead. They are exactly the same as the seven commands, but he stresses what followers of Jesus will experience—namely, how God will change toward them when they choose to give him a try.

The seven general commands aren't listed like this in the Bible, so you are free to change the list. Dropping the list, though, will mean those you are helping to follow Jesus will likely just continue to gain head knowledge and will not seek to implement what they learn. So it's a handy tool. Baby believers understand the commands at one level, while mature believers are still working to live them out fully in their lives at a different level. They are useful for those who are both young and old in the Lord.

The seven general commands are:

1. Repent and believe
2. Baptize
3. Break bread
4. Love
5. Pray (in the name of Jesus)
6. Give
7. Go

Bible study is the foundation to the list and undergirds it. Bible study is not an end goal. It's simply a means to an end. Getting to know Jesus really well is the goal! And that's a nice goal, isn't it?

5 Little Pictures

THE BIG PICTURE ON THE LITTLE PICTURES

So we looked at how to draw stick figures. We looked at some individual elements that are really simple. Here we will look at how to combine those happy little stick figures into a picture that illustrates a story. This means that you will get to become an illustrator, which sounds a whole lot better than becoming a stick figure-r. (That's even too hard to say!)

Two very different situations:

INFORMAL

FORMAL

Napkin Pics

Big Pics

There are two kinds of situations in which you will want to become a Story Ninja. One of them is informal. This is the one in which you are hanging out with your friends, enemies, or acquaintances. Maybe you are in a coffee shop or in a home or at the park with the kids. Maybe you've stopped on the bike trail or you're taking a break from running. (Please, do not attempt to become an illustrator while riding your bike or running or driving or doing a whole host of generally move-y things. That's dangerous!) Perhaps you are even out on the street meeting people, praying for the sick, and telling Jesus stories to individuals. That's more formal, but still in the informal category.

In these situations, it would be a bit weird to show up with your pictures already drawn, so instead grab a napkin or get out a notebook and draw one picture to tell the story. It might be a personal Jesus story or a biblical Jesus story. But you will begin and end with one small, probably very messy and convoluted, picture that you draw while you tell the story. These are the *little pictures*.

The other situation in which you might become a Story Ninja is one in which you are leading a group of people who are studying Bible stories together using pictures. This situation is more formal and will require a more formal setup. These pictures will generally be drawn big so that a group of people can see them. They might even be scanned and put onto a projector screen so that lots of people can see them. These pictures are usually drawn in scenes, each one on a different piece of paper or on different slides. These are what I have cleverly called the *big pictures*. (If it makes you feel more like a real artist, you could call them *les grandes images* in French, but we will stick with English here.)

It is totally OK to draw on napkins, with one really huge caveat: Do not use Grandma's Christmas napkins that are cloth with a pretty picture and are all intricately folded into a swan shape! Grandma will not be happy, and she will not want to hear any of your stories. When we mention a napkin here, we are picturing the ones at my house or in a fast-food restaurant. They are cheap paper napkins. You can draw on them and then either throw them away or keep them. Don't draw on cloth napkins.

How people look when you draw pictures on their cloth napkins:

Just to be clear, little pictures do not *have* to be drawn on napkins. They could be drawn on (gasp!) paper, a piece of wood, sand, dirt, an iPad screen, the dust on top of your dresser because you never listen when your mother tells you to dust, or any number of other dusty places. Any of those mediums will do for little pictures. Everyone knows that the truly great artists work in many different mediums. So the more different things you draw on (as long as it's not cloth napkins!), the better.

Picture this: You and your friends are chatting away, and the conversation goes deeper than cookies (yum!). You begin to have some authentic discussion and relationship. One of your friends mentions a problem. You care for your friend and want to help them, so you decide to tell them a Jesus story from your own life.

There are just a few social skills that will be needed before you share a Jesus story:

1. Express empathy for your friend and how hard it must be for them.

2. Don't equate your story or experience to your friend's. Say that it's similar, but acknowledge that it's not totally the same. No two situations are exactly alike.

3. Don't enter into a competition with your friend. For example, if he or she is worried about paying a two-hundred-dollar bill, don't say, "That's nothing! I have to trust God for thousands of dollars all the time. You'll be fine." Problems are not a competition to be won; they are to be acknowledged with empathy.

4. Share a story—not generalizations or principles. Share a specific time God provided—not that God generally provides.

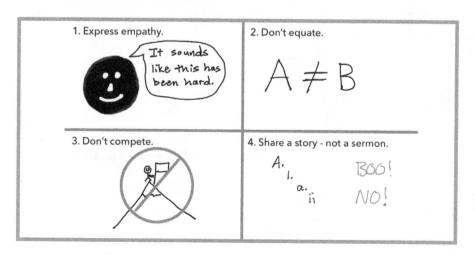

THE LITTLE PICTURE ON THE LITTLE PICTURES

Assuming that you have done those things, then you begin your story. Below you will see what you, the storyteller, would say on the right side, and the little "napkin" drawings will be on the left side.

In this first story, I will tell a personal testimony (also known as a personal Jesus story). These stories are often bypassed when we think of storytelling, but they are powerful. And they are super easy to tell because *you* were there when they happened! So there's not much to do in the way of memorization or learning. Now that's pretty awesome, for sure.

So here you go with a personal Jesus story told out loud (but in print on the right for you), with napkin drawing samples on the left.

"When I first moved here, I didn't have a job or any friends."

"I'd go for interviews, but people were mean to me, even though I was qualified for the jobs."

"As I was praying one day, the Lord said to me, 'I provide favor when you need it. I'll give you favor at this next interview.'"

"So, I went in, and as soon as the lady laid eyes on me, she just seemed to like me."

"She offered me the job, and it's been a pretty good job so far."

Do you notice how very simple these drawings are? Most people don't have enough time or brain power to tell the story and to draw amazing and complicated pictures at the same time. Anyway, the pen usually doesn't work very well on the napkin. The napkin usually slips or gets ripped or something like that. So keep the pictures simple and easy.

Also notice that you might only have one napkin, so you have to economize space and plan ahead. If your first picture takes up the whole napkin, then that can make it hard to finish the story well. So start off in just one little area. Finally, have your pictures follow the pattern that the local culture reads in. So for most of the languages you know, that will mean starting in the upper left-hand corner of your napkin and having your picture flow from left to right.

That's not too complicated with a personal story, but what about a biblical story? I thought you'd never ask. ...

BIBLE STORIES ON A NAPKIN

There are a couple of "classic" Bible stories that end up getting told over and over again. One of those Bible stories is the story of a wayward, wild son who runs off and spends his inheritance before his father is even dead (Luke 15:11–32). This story is usually called "The Prodigal Son" in those headlines that later editors added to our Bibles.

The story of the wild child (aka the prodigal son) is one of Jesus' parables. Knowing that it's a parable is important because a parable is a story that never actually happened. This means that the characters in the story are not actual historical people. A parable is a story that Jesus made up to prove a point. Jesus did a lot of that. In fact, some of the all-time favorite Jesus stories for most people are parables: made-up stories that never actually happened but are useful for teaching about God and his kingdom.

So imagine sitting in a restaurant with loud people all around you and the remains of a really tasty meal on your plate. You and your friend start talking about real-life stuff: struggles at work, in marriage, with kids, and in finances. You encourage your friend to ask Jesus to help with life's problems, and your friend says, "I don't think God is really interested in helping someone like me."

You say, "I believe that Jesus knew you would be here with me one day, questioning yourself and having this conversation with me. For this very moment, Jesus told a story. I would like to tell it to you now, because I'm pretty sure you will find it encouraging."

The story of the wild child can be a bit complicated as a napkin story, but one attempt to tell the story is illustrated below. Once again, the napkin drawings are on the left and what the Story Ninja is saying out loud is on the right.

"There was a man with two sons."

"The younger son wanted his inheritance before the father died, and the father agreed."

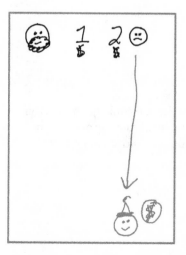

"As soon as he got his money, the younger son took off and left home. He partied and spent all of his money."

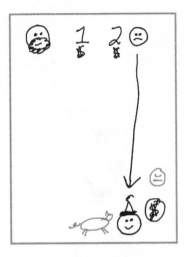

"He was totally broke and no one would help him. So, he got a job taking care of pigs and he was tempted to eat their food because he was so hungry."

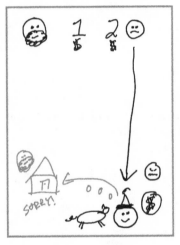

"One day he thought: Even the servants at home are better off than me. Maybe if I go home and apologize and admit I was wrong and beg my dad for a job, he'll hire me. So, he headed towards home, hoping his dad would let him be a servant."

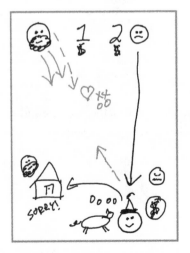

"But long before the son could get home, the dad saw him and went running out to him. The dad was hugging and kissing his lost son."

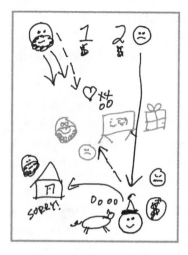

"The son apologized and admitted he'd messed up. But the dad told the servants to go prepare a big feast and to bring great gifts to the son to celebrate."

"The dad then said: My son was dead but now he is alive! And the party began. There's more to the story later, but I'll stop there for now."

Once again, the pictures are very simple. When telling stories like this one, the pictures can end up being quite complex before you know it. Keeping the pictures simple can be very hard!

Savvy Bible scholars will recognize that there is still a very important scene in this story that I haven't even gotten to. Sometimes stories need to be presented in stages so that people can receive them in stages. In this case, if the main point (Tool #1 – The Bow and Arrow) is to show people that God longs for them to come back to him, then this much of the story is enough. On the other hand, if you want to tell a story about the dangers and futility of jealousy in the kingdom, then the story will need to continue. It all depends on why the story is being told.

Note that the story did end with a teaser that there was more to be had of the story later on. It's good to let people know when there is more. They just might end up asking you to finish the rest of the story once you've given them some time to digest part of the story.

When the story is over, it's good just to stop and pause for a moment. You can take a sip of your drink while the story sinks in. Perhaps (gasp!) some thinking might even happen! After this pause, you might ask a simple follow-up question or two, such as, "What did you think of that story? Based on the story, how do you feel about God right now?"

Most people will already realize that God is like the father in the story. But if they haven't, you might need to help them with that concept. Still, it's best not to preach the story, but to ask people what they understand from the story and what parts stand out to them. Then see where the Holy Spirit wants to take the moment from there. We will talk more later about further questions you might ask or where you might want to go from here, especially if this turns into a good conversation.

For now, that's how to draw simple stick figures on a napkin to share Jesus stories with one or two people in an informal situation. Why not stop now to ask Jesus for an opportunity to share a simple stick-figure story with someone in the near future? Then take a minute to think through what personal or biblical stories you might want to share with someone, if the opportunity should arise.

THE REAL DEAL

Perhaps praying for an opportunity sounds great in some sort of abstract *Star Trek* time warp or on some other interdimensional planet, but it sounds crazy in real life. That's often the case with things that a person has never personally experienced. Rest assured that when God's people pray for opportunities to share the Good News and listen to God's voice, then opportunities will arise.

Sometimes things don't happen just because people have never done them before. For example, my friend keeps reminding me of the first time I was ever crazy enough to go jogging. She reminds me of how hot and sweaty and pink I was when I came back from being outside. She said, "Wow! How far did you jog?"

I answered, "I actually ran for exactly three minutes."

She seemed shocked since I had been gone for more than thirty minutes. But I had to build up to it slowly. That night, I groaned and complained about the pain I was in. But I kept building those muscles and eventually ran the world's slowest half-marathon.

We can all grow and get better. Maybe each of us will work our way up to the spiritual equivalent of running or walking a 5K, just over three miles (or finally making it to the end of the block!), rather than sitting on the couch. Maybe we will never be as awesome as that one person we know who just seems to be a natural at this whole "sharing Jesus" thing. That doesn't mean we shouldn't try.

I think Jesus actually told a parable about what happens to people who don't try! The New Living Translation calls it the Parable of the Three Servants, but it has traditionally been known as the Parable of the Talents (Matt 25:14–30). Let's pretend that you and I are sitting across the table from each other and the Lord prompts me to tell this story to you. It would go something like this:

"There was a boss about to go on a trip. He gave one of his employees five bags of money, one guy he gave two bags, and to one guy he gave one bag of money."

"The guy with five bags of money invested it and got five bags more. The one with two bags got two more. But the third guy just dug a hole and buried the money."

"When the boss came back, they each showed him what they had done with the money. He was happy with the first two and gave them better jobs and even gave them a celebration!"

"The third guy said that he was so afraid of messing up and losing the money that he didn't do anything. The boss called him 'wicked' and 'lazy' and took away all of his money."

The one thing that's not allowed in this story is simply to bury Jesus' gifts. The other thing that is not permitted in the parable is to compare ourselves to those who are really good at something. Everyone who tried their best got the same party from the boss.

Imagine what would happen if people gave up after they tried something new only one time. No one would ever become proficient at anything! It's very likely that all of us would feel awkward and unnatural at first. The way to get past that is to keep going until a familiarity settles in and muscle memory is built.

THE STORY OF ALICE, BETTY, YOU, AND JESUS

To help you imagine what telling Jesus stories over coffee might look like in a real-life scenario, let's look at the following story. (Maybe you should get a cookie as you settle into this great story. Just a thought.)

"There was a king that didn't know God and was super arrogant. He thought he had built his whole kingdom by himself."

"God saw how arrogant he was and made the bad king go live like an animal in the wilderness."

"Eventually, the king realized he'd messed up and got humble. He finally gave God credit. When he did, God gave him his kingdom back."

Daniel 4:28–37

Alice got a chance to tell a story from the Bible to Betty because she prepared each day and also because she asked the Lord to help her love her friend well. If we do these things too, we will get to share stories about Jesus too.

HELPFUL BITS

Which Stories Do I Tell?
Ones That Help Us to Obey!

There are parts of the Bible, other than stories, that can also be quoted or shared to help people follow the seven general commands of Jesus. Since we are focusing on stories, this list doesn't include any Scriptures from Paul or the Psalms—only the story parts of the Bible. All parts of the Bible are good, but the focus of this book is on the stories.

Basic Command	A Few Possible Bible Stories
1. Repent and believe	• Zacchaeus—Luke 19:1–10 • Jonah (but no big fish)—Jonah 3 • Nicodemus—John 3:1–21 • Philippian jailer—Acts 16:25–34 • Passover—Exodus 12:1–13 (Points forward) • Moses and the plague of snakes—Numbers 21:4–9 (points forward) • Parable of the prodigal son—Luke 15:11–32
2a. Baptize— Water baptism	• Lydia—Acts 16:11–15 • Ethiopian eunuch/official—Acts 8:26–40 • Jesus—Mark 1:9–11 • Philippian jailer—Acts 16:25–34 • Noah and the flood was an Old Testament symbol of baptism, according to the New Testament—1 Peter 3:18–22 (can be told as more than one story)
2b. Baptize—Baptism in the Holy Spirit	• John the Baptist—Mark 1: 4–8 • Jesus and his disciples—Acts 1:4–11 • Day of Pentecost—Acts 2:1–12 • Peter defends his actions—Acts 11:1–18
3a. Breaking bread— Communion	• Paul tells the story—1 Corinthians 11:23–26 • The Last Supper—Mark 14:12–26

3b. Breaking bread—Fellowship	• Paul and Eutychus—Acts 20:7–12 (Clearly they met together a long time!) • New Testament body life—Acts 2:42–47
4a. Love—God	• Jesus and the teacher of the law—Mark 12:28–34 • Jesus—John 14:15–21 • Parable of the prodigal son—Luke 15:11–32 • Baal and false prophets—1 Kings 18:20–40 • Hosea—3:1–5
4b. Love—Neighbors	• Parable of the good Samaritan—Luke 10:25–37 • Gleaning in the fields—Leviticus 19:9–10 • Boaz and Ruth—Ruth 2:1–23
4c. Love—Other believers	• Jesus—John 15:12–14 • Widow feeds Elijah—1 Kings 17:8–16 • Jerusalem famine offering—Acts 11:27–30
4d. Love—Enemies	• Jesus—Matthew 5:43–48 • Jesus—Luke 6:27–36 • Jesus on the cross—Luke 23:32–43 • David spares Saul—1 Samuel 24:1–22 • Parable of the unforgiving servant—Matthew 18:21–35
5. Pray (intercession, worship, listening, spiritual warfare, healing, etc.)	• The Lord's Prayer—Matthew 6:5–14 • Parable of persistent widow—Luke 18:1–8 • Parable of Pharisee and tax collector—Luke 18:9–14 • Your Father gives good gifts—Matthew 7:7–11 • Jesus speaks—John 15:15–16 • Daniel prays—Daniel 6:10–28 • Cornelius' prayers were heard—Acts 10:6–8 • Jesus healed many—Mark 1:29–34

6. Give (time, talent, treasure, everything)	• Jesus says to give secretly—Matthew 6:1–4 • Parable of talents three servants—Matthew 25:14–30 • Parable of shrewd manager—Luke 16:1–13 • Parable of rich fool—Luke 12:13–21 • Don't be anxious—Luke 12:22–34 • Widow's offering—Luke 21:1–4 • Boy with bread and fish—John 6:1–13 • Widow feeds Elisha—1 Kings 17:8–16 • Zacchaeus—Luke 19:1–9
7. Go and make disciples (evangelism and missions)	• Great Commission—Matthew 28:16–20 • Parable of wedding banquet—Luke 14:12–24 • Missionary team—Acts 13:1–3 • Samaritan woman—John 4 • Man born blind—John 9 • Lazarus—John 12:9–11 • Jesus sends out disciples—Luke 10:1–24 • Jesus heals a demon-possessed man—Mark 5:1–20 • Saul's conversion—Acts 9:1–31 • Philip—Acts 8 • Abraham—Genesis 12:1–7 • Jesus and a rich man—Mark 10:17–27

When stories appear in more than one Gospel, I usually learn the one from Mark first. That's because his version of the stories is always the shortest!

Notice that not all of the stories are neat and easy stories. Maybe some of them are more advanced stories for more mature believers, but we should be aware of those too.

I know that some Christians don't like to talk about the baptism in the Holy Spirit because we have so many disagreements about it. However, Hebrews 6:1–3, according to the New Living Translation, includes "baptisms" as part of the "basic teachings about Christ." And the baptism in the Holy Spirit (not always with exactly the same wording) is mentioned in several different places in the Bible.

Some of the stories as referenced here are too long. You will need to share a summary of the story or break it into sections. I generally included the entire story here for context.

6 Big Pictures for Groups

PREP WORK

Get ready ... Get set ...

Don't go ... Not quite yet ...

Hold on there, pardner ...

We're gettin' there ...

Got some prep work to do before we hit the dusty trail ...

I'm just a stick figure cowboy, riding my horse. Or maybe it's a big dog. Who can tell? Anyway, slow down there, pardner!

There is another setting in which you might also get to tell Jesus stories. It's a more formal setting. These settings are when a group of people gathers with the expectation of learning more about Jesus. This could be a seeker's group, where people gather to see if they'd like to follow Jesus, a church meeting, a home group, a Bible study, or any other similar type of gathering.

In this kind of setting, I personally find it best to draw the pictures in advance and to work in advance to get ready for the Bible storytelling. I know a few people who can draw their pictures and tell the story at the same time, but that requires too much coordination and thought for me to do all at once. And it turns out that I'm not that abnormal. Most people want to draw the pictures in advance so that they can concentrate exclusively on telling the story when the time comes.

So before you can even draw the pictures, there is a lot of work to be done!

HOW TO GET READY TO DRAW PICTURES FOR A GROUP

How do you know which stories to pick? Well, there are lots of reasons to pick different stories. But the main idea here is to keep the main idea in mind! (Remember the bow and arrow?) What main point are you wanting people to know? If some of them are new to following Jesus, then you might want to help them realize that the first command of Jesus is to repent. So you would likely want to pick a story that would help people understand that. (There is more on that in some of the Little Bits sections of this book.)

On the other hand, perhaps some of the people are encountering a particular problem in life, so maybe you want to pick a story that would address that problem. (There's more on that in some of the Little Bits sections too!) Or perhaps you'd just like the people to understand the overall flow of the story of the Bible. In that case, you might choose to go chronologically through stories, so you simply pick the next story in the sequence. Perhaps Christmas or Easter is coming up, so it's time to study the related stories in the Gospels.

There is a wide variety of reasons to pick different stories at different times. The principles of the Story Ninja are still the same: determine the main goal of the study time and then pick a story that you think will help get you and your friends to that goal.

2. Divide the story into Parts

Many Bible stories are long—too long for one telling. For example, if you pick the stories of Abraham, Joseph, Moses, Jesus, Peter, Paul, etc., then the story of their life is too long for one telling. In general, a story that is a good length for using in a group will be about ten verses long. It won't take you very long to realize that ten verses is not very long at all!

Why keep the stories so short? The first reason is because your study group has never heard the story before. Now if your group knows the stories pretty well, then you can cover longer stories or even an overview of a *very* long story. However, keep in mind that it is rare to have a group in which *everyone* has advanced knowledge of the Bible. And it's not realistic to assume that *everyone* already knows the story.

The second reason to keep the stories short is when you are telling the story from memory in a language that is not your mother tongue or perhaps is *not* the mother tongue of the group you are working with. So if you have to learn the story in another language (e.g., if you are a missionary in another culture) or if the people are listening in a second language (like international students in your home culture or minorities using a national language), then ten verses can already feel rather long.

Keeping those two things in mind, then, let's think of ten verses as "about ten verses" or "somewhere in the neighborhood of ten verses" or "in the ballpark of ten verses." So it's not a hard and fast rule, but the idea is there. If you experiment (i.e., try things until you learn them), then you will figure out that short, in general, is better.

Once you have chosen your story (about ten verses) and divided it into parts (of about two to three verses each), then you have begun to outline the story in your mind. You've begun to notice changes of location or action or main characters. Perhaps you've noticed long dialogue or secondary characters who are there but don't do much.

Ultimately, you are thinking of drawing pictures of these four sections. Can you draw more than four pictures? Well, technically you can draw *four gazillion* pictures if you want! (Believe me, you don't want to. You really, really don't.) However, four pictures is easy to do on a standard piece of paper. And if you draw six pictures or eight or ten, then you will end up making the story harder to remember and you will begin to lose reproducibility.

Can you draw two pictures? Well, yes, if you want. It might not be a very exciting story, though, if there are only two pictures. Sometimes two pictures (or six) work fine, however. So experiment and see. In later sections of this book you will see some examples of guest drawers who violated some of my rules. I am still friends with those people, even though they broke the "rules"! So that tells you that these things are guidelines—not hard and fast rules.

3. Imagine the setting of the story in your mind. Picture the places and people in the story.

This brain is busy imagining. It's fun! You should try it!

Next, begin to notice people and places in the story. Notice the setting of the story. Does the story take place in a city, in the countryside, on a farm, in a rugged place, or in a tame place? Begin to ask yourself if it's hot or cold. Do you know?

What do the people in the story look like or smell like? Are they clean and wearing fancy clothes? Or are they dirty or hungry and wearing simple, even dirty, clothes?

Don't forget to notice crowds or servants or children or crowds who would also be a part of the stories. What are these secondary characters doing? How are they feeling? Are the main characters including these folks in their actions or doing certain things because of the "extra characters"? Like pushing through a crowd perhaps? Jesus often had crowds following him or around him, jeering at him or cheering for him.

How are each of the people in the story feeling? What is their attitude toward each other or Jesus? This will impact the way you draw their mouth and eyes. Ask yourself: Do these people like each other, or are they enemies? What are their hopes and dreams? Why are they even at this place at this time?

Spend time reading and re-reading (or listening and re-listening) to the story and thinking through the overall setting. Don't forget to imagine trees, animals, flowers, water, smells of people, food, sweat, flowers, etc.

4. Imagine the actions taking place in the story.

Next, begin to notice if people are walking or moving or simply standing around. Are people rowing boats, tossing nets, or doing other kinds of labor? If people are at the tabernacle or the temple, where are they? Are they standing or kneeling outside because they are women or Gentiles? What body positions are people in when they are praying? Are messengers coming and going? Are horses or donkeys stamping their hooves, or sheep shuffling around in their flocks?

Sometimes, for example, the disciples go off to do something (find food or lodging) and then come back. Sometimes whole crowds of people are waving palm fronds in the air or throwing them on the ground. Sometimes people are deliberately not looking someone else in the eye. Sometimes they are picking up stones, large ones, to throw at someone else. Notice and imagine all the actions and movements in the story you've chosen. Then choose wisely which details you want to include that help tell the story.

5. Practice drawing 3-4 pictures using these places, people, and actions.

It's finally time to make some rough drafts of your stories. This means that if you have some nice, big pieces of paper that you intend to use for your "real" pictures (so a group of people can all see them), then don't use them yet. Just get a scrap of paper or a patch of dirt and sketch out your stories. You are likely to find some sort of problem in your pictures at this point. For example, you might realize that you don't know how to draw porpoise skins. (Yes, they are in the Bible!) Or you might realize that you aren't sure how to draw some sort of action. Perhaps you'll realize that your story is too long and complicated. You might not have left enough room for the crowd. Anyway, making a rough draft is a good idea so that you don't ruin your big, fancy paper.

For the impatient types, I do realize that we haven't yet drawn one "official" picture. The prep work is good for the presentation, but it's also good for our souls. In the midst of all this prep work, hopefully the Holy Spirit spoke to you and you were speaking to him. It might even be that you are noticing new things about this story and that you and God are enjoying discovering his Word together. That would be really nice. So now we are finally about to go over some specific things to include in your pictures! So wait just a second or two and look over the next section before you pick up your pen and your big pieces of paper. The enthusiasm is good, though. Keep it up!

HOW TO DRAW PICTURES FOR A GROUP

OK, now that we got all of that preparatory thinking, studying, and praying done, I think you probably need a cookie. (Yum!) Cookies are good, so very good. And now you are probably ready to start actually drawing some pictures.

In this section we are preparing to share the stories with a group of people. This group may or may not include children. This technique was not designed with children in mind, but they do pretty well with it. In fact, kids may not need as much repetition as adults. Sometimes when people see the stick figures they assume this book is for the children's workers. Although children's workers will benefit from this technique, it is not primarily for them. Using this method in a church meeting can make it possible to keep kids and adults together for all or most of the time. This can lead to healthy discipleship across generations and can relieve the need for "childcare," where at least one adult misses the church meeting altogether.

Remember that these pictures are not being drawn just for your own entertainment, although you will be entertained. You are planning to show them to a group of people so that you can study the Bible together. Keep this in mind when deciding how big to make your pictures. If your groups are small and you visit a lot of homes (like missionaries often do), then keep your pictures small so they can fit in your bag and you will always have them with you.

If you are going to be in front of a home group, then your pictures might need to be a bit bigger, maybe 11 x 17 or something like that. For some large groups, we have put pictures on poster board so everyone can see them. And occasionally you might even need to project them on a gigantic screen through a computer system. That works too. The principle here is that people get cranky when the pictures are too small to be easily seen. And when people get cranky, that's not good.

Like all things, there are some good ways and some not-so-good ways to draw pictures. So here are seven super-duper simple steps to drawing pictures well.

1. Number four big pieces of paper. Each page will contain a picture of one of your "parts" that you chose earlier. You will mix up the pictures later, so this will help you get them back in order quickly. If you initially draw the pictures all on one piece of paper, then number each quadrant. Later you can rip the paper into four pieces.

2. Put the Scripture reference on the first picture. Why? It keeps you from having to look it up later. If you are just telling it to a friend, you might just say generally where the story is in the Bible. But if you are telling it in a church meeting, then this is very important. After all, you want them to learn where the story is and be able to look it up later if they want to do so.

3. Write out in detail in the local language any names of cities or people whenever they make their first appearance. This helps people who can read a bit learn and remember these terms.

4. If there is a lot of action to remember in one picture, put numbers or letters or symbols and arrows on the different action points in the pictures so you don't forget something.

5. Try to be aware of what order people read in within the culture. If the local text is left-to-right (like English), then the action of the pictures goes left-to-right. If the local text is right-to-left (like Arabic), then the action of the pictures goes right-to-left as well.

6. Try to put in some sort of symbol to help you remember the content of any dialogue. Use dialogue bubbles and symbols but not words. Try to keep the words as little as possible within the pictures.

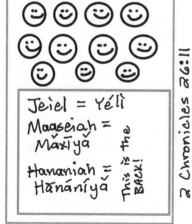

7. Make notes in words on the back of pictures. This is especially useful when you are telling the story in a language other than your mother tongue. You might get nervous and suddenly go blank. So, put a few key words you're struggling with on the back of the pictures. DO NOT write out the whole story, though. That's sort of defeating the point of learning to tell the stories from heart.

BAD OPTIONS. DON'T DO THESE THINGS. REALLY, DON'T.

Are you starting to wonder if the "simple process of telling Jesus stories" is not that simple anymore? It's true that it does take some thought and intentionality to draw stick figures that save the world. However, the steps are not difficult or complicated. You can do this.

Still, some of you might be tempted to do some things other than follow the easy instructions included so far in this book. For you, I am listing some things *not* to do below. I am listing them here because I know some of you will be sorely tempted by them. Flee temptation! Run from the dark side!

Bad Option A:
Going back to lecturing instead of using these oh so simple stick figures. Yes, lecturing might be initially easier for you, but it isn't reproducible.

Lecturing is easier sometimes than telling stories or making learning interactive. But easier is not always better. Most of what is told in lectures is not remembered. So don't give in to the temptation to go back to lecturing simply because it's easier. Although people sometimes claim to like lectures, they will embrace storytelling in the midst of the lecture. In fact, in most instances all they will remember later are the stories you told in the midst of the lecture. So resist the urge to backtrack to a less effective method.

Bad Option B:
Using someone else's pictures and not drawing your own. (After all, they look so much nicer anyway...)

Of all the things I've seen people do, this is the most common. It's so easy in the modern world to use someone else's pictures. You just get on the internet and find some pictures—and voila, it's done. The problem is that pictures that someone else drew bypass the thinking phases of this process. And it's the thinking phases that lead to the most fruit. When you draw your own pictures, you interact with the stories, you imagine them, you outline them, you produce them with your own hand. They might not look as nice in the end, but they are far better overall.

If you are working in a mission situation and you bring in preprinted materials that the locals don't have access to, then they will not go and tell stories if you don't give the pictures to everyone. Your preprinted pictures will create a bottleneck for the gospel, as people decide *not* to share the stories because there aren't enough of the pictures to go around. Creating your own simple pictures from local materials means there is always enough for everyone and there are less barriers to sharing the stories.

Bad Option C:
Using a recording of someone else telling the story rather than telling it from your own heart. (After all, they tell it so much better…)

There is nothing evil or wrong with recordings of people telling stories. However, that is not the point of what we are doing here. We are trying to learn to not be dependent on just a few professionals or just a few resources to have the Word of God run swiftly. The best way to see the gospel flow quickly is to make sure that every man, woman, and child has it embedded in their heart and are able to tell the Good News at any time. Using a video or having someone else tell the Good News recreates the bottleneck of relying on certain resources to be available. It also masks the fact that we don't know the stories of Jesus very well ourselves.

Don't keep yourself from having the privilege of knowing the Word of God very well by giving in to using videos *instead* of your own words and skills.

You can use the videos to help you get the stories into your own heart, but be ready—no matter where you are and no matter what materials you have available—to tell Jesus stories. The only way to do that is to have them in your own heart, which also makes them more heartfelt. Therefore, the stories are more loving and more likely to be received better by the listener when given by a live person.

Bad Option D:
Using this book as a fire starter on a cold winter's night. (After all, it was meant to start a fire for Jesus in the hearts of humans…)

OK, so that's just crazy. Don't do it. There surely must be something better you can do with this book! You could at least laugh at the pictures, perhaps …

Bad Option E:
Hurting your hand so that you can get out of drawing pictures or otherwise claiming you are not physically up to the task. (Come on, it's not THAT bad!)

The pain of drawing pictures is *surely* less than the pain of a broken hand. And a broken hand is inconvenient for so many other reasons. Just try to draw a picture or two. You'll see that it's not that horrible. On a scale of horribleness, drawing pictures must be less than a 4 out of 10, am I right? There are way worse things.

LET THE MEETING BEGIN. PREPPING YOUR PEOPLE.

Adults were also made for story. This is one of the reasons why adults like to watch movies and television. However, many adults will recoil at the thought of using childish stick figures. So the first thing is to put their fears at bay and let them give this whole thing a try. Although the pictures are simple, the meaning of the stories is rich and deep. Don't let the stick figures push people away.

The main group that has struggled with this technique is older believers who are used to traditional Bible studies. So they will probably need a little help to get used to the idea. Traditional Bible studies don't require as much work or engagement with the story as this approach does. As a result, some traditional believers don't like to have to work so hard. Sometimes they also get embarrassed because they discover that they don't know their Bible as well as they thought. It's OK, you can help them through it.

To give you some ideas on how to help people get used to this new way of Bible study, I have created our very own Choose Your Own Adventure Story (How cool is that?). Read below, choose your solution, and see the outcome.

You see your church member's thoughts (so you like already have superpowers in this story!), so you:

    A. Give up and go back to old methods

    B. You charge on ahead with no explanation

    C. Empathize and explain

Choose one of these adventure options and see the outcome below!

LET THE STORY BEGIN!
HOW TO ACTUALLY TELL A STORY IN A MEETING

You've chosen your story.

You've drawn your story.

You've practiced your story.

Now you're almost ready!

Remember, you don't have to have it memorized, but you should know it so well that some sections are almost word for word from the Bible now. The last step is to explain to your group that you'll be sharing with them using simple pictures that anyone could draw so that they will be able to remember it better and share it with others.

Many believers know that Christ should be shared, but too often they don't apply that call to themselves. Telling them your reasoning in your opening explanation should spark something in them. Now it's time to tell the story to the group. At last!

The method described here is one way to tell the story a lot and still not get bored with it. To make it all the way through this process takes at least an hour. If time is tight, less can be done, but less will likely be learned as well. And less life transformation will happen. It would be nice to think that people will go home and study the story, but they likely won't. So we study together in a group so that everyone can learn the story.

With traditional believers who have been in Bible study or church a long time, I make them close their Bibles and just listen to the story. This is not because I think that reading the Bible is wrong. Of course, the more we read our Bibles, the better. However, when they sit and read it, they don't listen well and they don't work on getting it into their hearts. They just keep looking at the words on the page and sometimes looking at other stuff that catches their eye. I have found that people pay attention and learn the one story we are working on better, if they close their Bibles and listen attentively. You might need to review the pep talks above, if your group is really resistant to this!

So this story has these guys called Pharisees. They were super strict about religious things. They thought they were better than everyone else. They even looked down on Jesus for things he did.

1. Introduce the story by explaining anything that might be weird, unusual, or confusing to your audience.

And now the story begins ....

...And that's the end of the story.

2. Tell the story. Clearly mark the beginning and end of the story.

WORLD'S MOST TEMPTING CHOCOLATE BAR

LORD, HELP ME!

3. Resist the temptation to explain the story. Remember, you will get to the meaning of the story later when you ask the "Discovery Bible Study" questions.

4. Point to each of your pictures and ask questions. But just ask about the facts—not the meaning! Use words like *who*, *what*, *when*, *where*, and *how*.

5. Tell the story again. Clearly mark the beginning and the end.

6. Pass out one picture to different people. Have them hold the picture and tell what happened in their picture. Help them tell the story, if they need it.

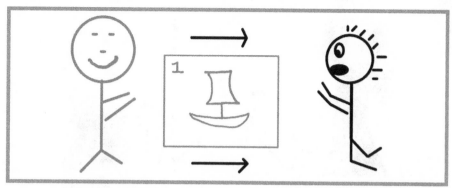

7. Let each person who just told part of the story pass on their picture to someone else. Now, the second person to hold that picture will also tell the portion of the story in that picture.

8. Ask if there is one brave soul who would be willing to tell the story from beginning to end using the pictures.

9. Now encourage your group to be bold and draw their own version of the story. Let them use their Bibles and read the story while they draw their own pictures, if they are able to do so.

10. Now do the "Discovery Bible Study" part of the meeting. Ask your group: What do you learn about humans? What do you learn about God/Jesus? What should we do about what we learned?

11. Tell the group to find a partner and take turns sharing the story with their partner.

12. When the group is finished sharing their stories with each other, call the group together and encourage them to take a few minutes to pray. They should ask Jesus for a chance to tell the story to other people and to have their own life changed by the story.

13. Ask the group to turn back to their partner and finish the phrase, "As a result of what I learned here today, I will ..." Have each person share their "I will" statements with someone else and then pray for each other.

That's a long process and can be tiring. It's important to make sure that the drawing time is relaxed and fun. Snacks help with this. Well, snacks (like cookies, for example) make most everything better. Limit the amount of time people have to draw pictures. If you don't, some people will set out to create something worthy of a museum—especially if they are good at drawing. About fifteen minutes or less is enough for most groups to draw their pictures, stretch, and chat without losing them altogether.

People in some cultures are taught to be creative from childhood. For example, American children are encouraged *not* to copy someone else but to show their own creativity instead. Such cultures sometimes have people who are a bit *too* creative, and they might stray from the biblical text. If they do, encourage them to draw their pictures their way, but to stay true to the story.

On the other hand, some cultures are taught that mimicry is best. In these cultures, people often try to copy the teacher's pictures exactly. Be aware of this. If you are a teacher from outside the culture, test your pictures with a small group of locals before using them too widely. Pictures are read differently from culture to culture, and you will need to check them the same way you might check any Bible translation.

When people ask if they can see your pictures to copy them, go ahead and let them do so. Not all cultures or individuals like to be creative. Some just want to do it "right." This is fine if they do this. The main thing is that they copy the pictures by hand (rather than taking out their cell phone and just snapping a photo). The copying process is the study process. Copying a picture embeds the story in our brains as if we watched it happen.

If they want to take a photo too, that's fine. The main thing is not to bypass the learning. In fact, many people do take photos of their pictures and then have them on their phone. This helps to make sure that the pictures are always with them and handy.

Keep the environment light and encouraging throughout. If people get answers wrong or really mess it up, always thank them for being brave! Then work on gently bringing some correction. If people feel embarrassed, they might not want to come to church anymore.

It also helps that I, the teacher, have sometimes had an epic fail in front of the growing disciples. When I do, I apologize and ask them to help me. I try to avoid these, but mistakes also make me real and human. I get really nervous sometimes when I get up to tell a story for the first time. I've been known to go blank altogether for a second or two. This is OK. I have found that it has helped people to see that I do value getting the stories accurate, that I value the Word of God, and that I mess up, but then live to tell the tale. Basically, Jesus is gracious enough to work with even the likes of you and me. Now that's good news!

7 Next Steps

You are now officially deputized and authorized to go become a Jesus story superhero. Jesus will always be the star of the show (which is a huge relief!), but you have a role to play too. Here is your badge.

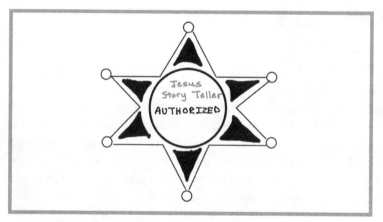

You can pin it on your chest and let people know that this is your job and this is what you do. Why? *Because Jesus people tell Jesus stories. That's what Jesus people do.*

Based on my very extensive knowledge of ninjas, I have figured out that they have to work out every day to stay in shape. Us Story Ninjas will need to work out every day too. This means practicing and reviewing a lot. It's how we stay ready for any opportunity that the Lord presents us with. I know that there are only like three people on the whole planet earth who *like* to work out, but we do it because we like what happens afterwards.

This whole no-one-really-likes-to-practice thing means that it will help if there is a group of Story Ninjas (your friends, family, church, small group, etc.) that get together to practice. You could make it a goal to learn a new story each week (or every two weeks or every day). You can draw the pictures, practice on your own, then get together to hold each other accountable and practice with each other.

You could even eat cookies while you do this! What other workout system recommends the use of cookies while working out? None that I know of, which automatically proves the superiority of this system, of course.

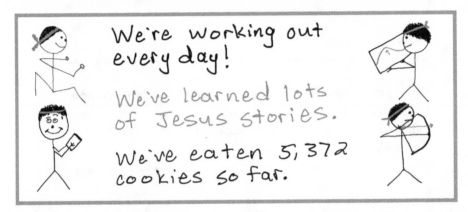

It is super fun if your Story Ninja group has people of all ages in it. Young, old, and middle-aged can all participate and learn together. This is a great way for adults to learn the Bible, but it works with kids too. Amazing! When kids and adults do this together, the adults even get it right eventually. I've drawn pictures with kids, adults, PhDs, senior citizens, international students working on their fifth language, people who solve cancer for a living, new believers, old believers, and nonbelievers. All of them learned to love and obey Jesus better as a result. I believe you will too.

Appendix A

SAMPLE DRAWINGS

In this appendix, I will share some of my own stick-figure drawings that I have done in many places and at different times. You will see that there is some variation in my style, depending on how I was feeling that day, what materials were available, and what language I was working in. Hopefully these samples will help give you some more helpful examples.

I have organized them around the seven general commands of Jesus, just so you see how those work. Many stories can be used for more than one command. Also, there are many more stories that could be used to represent each of these commands. These are just the ones I seem to like best!

You will notice that some of my stories are longer than four pictures. These were ones that I generally had put into my own notebook of personal quiet times. I feel free to be more expansive in my own quiet times than when I am trying to help others learn the Bible. Also, you will notice lines on some of the pages. Those are the lines in my notebook.

You might also notice that I even gave you a couple of examples of how to draw stick figures for some parts of the Bible that are not stories. It can be done, and it's just as useful as drawing pictures for the stories.

I am generally working from the New Living Translation, so if you want to follow along most closely with my symbols, that is the Bible translation you will want to use. However, any translation ought to work.

Command 1. Repent and Believe—Zacchaeus (Luke 19:1–10)

Command 1. Repent and Believe—John the Baptist (Mark 1:14–15)

Command 2. Baptize—Philip and the Ethiopian Eunuch (Acts 8:26–40)

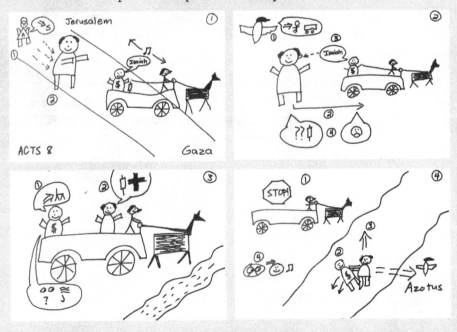

Command 3. Break Bread—The Last Supper (1 Corinthians 11:23–26)

Command 4. Love (God)—Tower of Babel (Genesis 11:1–9)

Command 4. Love (Neighbors, Enemies)— Unforgiving Servant (Matthew 18:21–25)

Command 4. Love (Enemies)—How to Treat Your Enemies (Romans 12:20–21)

Command 5. Pray—Don't Be Afraid to Speak to God (Exodus 20:18–21)

Command 5. Pray—Uzziah Sought the Lord (2 Chronicles 26:1–15)

Command 6. Give—Leave Some for Others (Leviticus 19:9–10)

Command 6. Give—Elisha Gives and Receives (Leviticus 19:9–10)

Command 7. Go—Jesus Sends out His Disciples (Luke 10:1–20)

Appendix B

SAMPLE DRAWINGS FROM OTHERS

The following are samples of Jesus Stories that many people have drawn at different times and in different places. This way you can see some other styles of drawing. Do *not* just photocopy these. Taking the time to draw your own pictures will get your brain juices pumping and get you thinking about Jesus. When you think about Jesus, you grow closer to him. Now, that's nice, isn't it?

Zacchaeus (Luke 19:1–10)
Thanks, Lisa Smart, for sharing! Used with permission.

Jesus Anointed by a Sinful Woman (Luke 7:36–50)
Thanks, Esther Wang, for these great pictures. Used with permission.

The Wide and Narrow Gate (Matthew 7:13–14)
Thanks to my buddy, Brett Mason, for this illustration. Used with permission.

The Feeding of the Five Thousand (Mark 6:33–44)
Thanks to Jean Nies for these nice drawings. Used with permission.

The picture below was drawn by Miriam, Jean's two-year-old. She was "helping" Mommy draw Jesus stories and then cut them into shreds with scissor practice. Just trying to let you know what real life is like.

Church at Antioch (Acts 11:19–30)
Thanks to Meredith Johnson for these. She is a true Story Ninja!
Used with permission.

Jesus Calms the Storm (Luke 8:22–25)
Thank you, Lisa Smart, for these very smart pictures. Used with permission.

Creation (Genesis 1:1–31)
Thanks to Matt Wallin for these pictures. Used with permission.

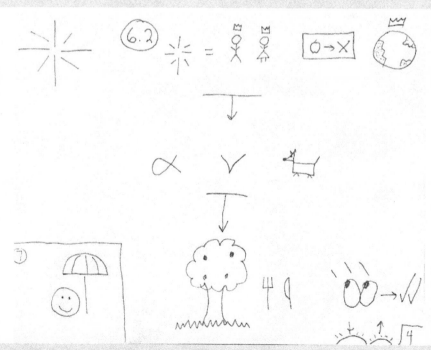

137

The Early Church (Acts 2:36–47)
Thanks to Peggy Spiers for these great pictures! Used with permission.

And that's how it's done!